Plan BE

"*Plan Be* takes the reader from a superficial, task-oriented view of our Christianity to an understanding that our peace and rest come only in "*Be*-ing" in Christ. Denny Hanrahan shows us that our striving for God's rest and security ultimately leads to trusting in self rather than the only one who can provide true peace and comfort.

Denny's focused objectives and journal guide for *Plan Be* leads believers to a deeper relationship with Christ—a relationship of being with, and in, our Lord and Savior."

Brett Billups – Human Resources Executive
and author of *Biblical HR*

"I pay close attention to the stories of men and women who demonstrate uncommon resilience, growth, and wisdom, despite difficult life circumstances. Denny Hanrahan is one of those people. His book takes you "under the hood" so you can understand how his personal "internal combustion engine" has functioned so well throughout the stages of life. I not only read about Denny's Be-attitudes, but I exercised them for myself and found my mind renewed, my connection with God deepened, and my attitude lifted. I highly recommend this book and utilizing the Be-attitudes as part of your spiritual workout routine."

Colonel Eric R. Bents – USAF (Ret)

"I love the fact that *Plan Be* is not a "feel-good book" . . . I'd call it a "feel-more challenge." Denny Hanrahan weaves his personal story in with Christ's messages to us . . . giving real-life examples of where God's words offer hope and solace. This is not a book you read; it is a book you *embrace*."

Jeff Lovejoy – Chief Relationship Officer, LAM Technology

"Take the challenge to live a God-honoring, character-developing life laid out in Plan Be. In a time of such personal confusion and the fabric of society unraveling, in Plan Be, Denny Hanrahan sets forth a worthy life trajectory, along with helpful pathways to get there. Denny reminds us that character counts and doing flows from our being. A desperately needed book for our times with real-life tools for anyone up to the challenge."

Dr. Will McRaney – President, Bullock Institute
(www.bullockinstitute.com)

"Most of us are living out what we would consider our 'Plan A' for our lives. Often when Plan A fails, we fall back on our Plan B. Either way, it is our plan, crafted by ourselves to get where we think we need to be. Sometimes we even varnish the plan with the thought that God somehow is encouraged and helped by us living out 'our own plan.' Denny Hanrahan takes a different approach, based on his own story and experience. He wants us to consider Plan Be, which is being willing to hear God and live out His plan for our lives. You must read this book!!"

Chuck Bryant – CEO, Pinnacle Forum America

"God calls us to a life of simple faith amidst the chaos and over-whelm in our world. I love how Denny shares how to overcome the 'Plan-A' life of pushing through the performance-driven world of doing, to a life of simply being, and trusting in God's ways as we walk with Him in intimacy."

Bob Lotich – Best-selling Author of *Simple Money, Rich Life* and Host of the *SeedTime Money Podcast*

PLAN BE

7 Be-Attitudes for Walking with God in Complete Trust and Freedom

Denny Hanrahan

NASHVILLE

NEW YORK • LONDON • MELBOURNE • VANCOUVER

PLAN BE

Seven Be-Attitudes for Walking with God in Complete Trust and Freedom

© 2023 Denny Hanrahan

Published in New York, New York, by Morgan James Publishing. Morgan James is a trademark of Morgan James, LLC. www.MorganJamesPublishing.com

Proudly distributed by Ingram Publisher Services.

To order additional books: www.plan-be-book.com

ISBN 9781631959929 paperback
ISBN 9781631959936 ebook
Library of Congress Control Number:
2022940951

Cover Design by:
Christopher Kirk
www.GFSstudio.com

Interior Design by:
Chris Treccani
www.3dogcreative.net

Editorial by:
Inspira Literary Solutions
Gig Harbor, WA

Morgan James is a proud partner of Habitat for Humanity Peninsula and Greater Williamsburg. Partners in building since 2006.

Get involved today! Visit MorganJamesPublishing.com/giving-back

*"Before the Lord wills me to do anything,
He first of all wills me to 'be.' What I do
must depend on who I am."*
~ Thomas Merton

*"It is not what we do that determines who we are;
it is who we are that determines what we do."*
~ Neil Anderson and Robert Saucy, *The Common Made Holy*

TABLE OF CONTENTS

BENEFACTORS

It all began with a bag of pens . . .

And Bill and Patti Johnson's Home Group. As leaders, they supplied everyone with writing journals that we'd use to jot down notes from our Bible studies. I still have many of these journals, and thanks to "B and P," I haven't stopped journaling. In those days, we'd bring pens to write with, but we'd inevitably misplace them or just plain forget to bring any. Bill and Patti started collecting them in what we ended up affectionately naming the "Bag o' Pens" and handing them out to whoever needed one.

In reflecting on this book, where it all started, and on all who've enriched my life along the way, I feel like each of those I've written about here has reached into the proverbial Bag o' Pens and indelibly inscribed their care and love in the journal of my heart.

Bill and Patti, without you, this writing would've never made the trip from brain to page. Thank you for kicking off my life of journaling and the journey to *Plan Be*, but, more importantly, for your love and prayers over the years. I love you two dearly!

To our Home Group friends: The Holdens, Beckers, Dardens, Aikens, Roses, and a list of neighbors too long to count. Thanks for your beautiful fellowship!

To the Giles Clan – Bob, Jansen, Clay, Jake, and Kevin. Thanks for showing us how a loving team works.

Kevin and Dori Gallagher: You are dear family; oh, the joy we've shared over the years!

Kyle and Melissa Johnson: I watch in awe at your unrestrained obedience to God. You are truly amazing!

To my Pinnacle Forum Brothers: Eric Bents, Brett Billups, Chuck Bryant, Cole Campbell, Stephen Casey, Brian DeMarco, Connor Hilliard, Jason Hooley, Chuck Klein, Doug McCrabb, Mike Monreal, and Rich Schaus. Each of you has deeply permeated my soul with your unparalleled gladness and service to Jesus. Your fellowship has been pure gold.

To Brett Billups and Cole Campbell: Thank you for taking the time to bushwhack through my rough draft and provide wise counsel. I treasure your friendship and wisdom!

To Bryan Ward, Anthony Johnson, Larry McQuay, Steve Ashton, Dan Barrett, and my brothers of 50 Bold: You're the iron that sharpens iron. Thank you for reminding me that dreams can come true, and then showing me how it's done.

To Dave Buzon, Greg Corner and Dave Trcka: We've shared countless moments of laughter. No one embodies the Be Joyful Be-Attitude more fully than you. I thank God for our lifelong friendship!

To Kery Maddox and Patrick O'Hara: Thanks for keeping the spirit of music alive in my life! I treasure our bond and always long to see you. Seems to me, it's chemistry!

Thanks to Arlyn Lawrence, Heather Sipes, and the team at Inspira Literary Solutions for your expertise in navigating this complex world of words. You've been amazing at seeing the big picture and translating my heart onto the pages. Without you, there'd simply be no *Plan Be*.

Thanks to Dennis Trittin at Lifesmart Publishing. You opened the literary door to me and then showed me through the next one, and for that, I'm eternally grateful.

To the team at Morgan James Publishing: Thank you for helping turn a concept in to something that the world can hold.

Jim and Missy Neathery: There isn't a finer example of unshakeable faith than what I've observed in your lives; I am honored to call you friends. Jim—the wisest man I know, you're victorious as a leader in spirit and truth.

To John Rose: I have no dearer friend on the planet. Your profound love for God is unmatched. Ruth Ann Rose, you are a portrait of strength and joy (and amazing wit!). I love you both beyond words!

To Joey and Michelle Hutto: Your love, hospitality, and beautiful respites at "Chateau Hutto" have been like a secret garden to me. You've refreshed my soul countlessly over the years.

To my sibs Lori Pettit, Sue Ashwill, Jim, and Dan Hanrahan: each of you has shown me throughout our life together that nothing can stop us. I'm deeply grateful for our special bond—we are conquerors! Our strength is steel, our love for each other eternal. And to all our better halves! Perry, Jeff, Amy, and Jane, you have added profound depth and meaning to our lives.

Mom and Bob Wallner: The pillars of our family, your love for each other and each of us is what makes a family, family. Mom, your eternal optimism has taught me how to overcome life's challenges with hope and positivity. You are the example!

Danny: My built-in best friend! I've looked up to you with awe my entire life. I'm so blessed to share it with the kindest (and funniest) person on the planet. I praise God for you continually.

John Hanrahan: You are my warrior and my champion. Your courage and boldness and your passion to live victoriously inspires me to be my best. Great things are in store for you!

Georgia Hanrahan: You're our beautiful model of grace and strength. How you demonstrate calm and steady confidence in life is poetry. You are simply amazing. I look forward to seeing how your excellent life unfolds!

Jill Hanrahan: You are my person! Because of you, I know soulmates are real. No one has loved or supported me better in this project and life than you have. Your exuberance for life—your sunshine joy—has inspired me deeply. Thanks for helping me be me. You are the reason for this book. I love you so much!

"'I know the plans I have for you,' declares the LORD, 'plans for welfare and not for evil, to give you a future and a hope" (Jeremiah 29:11, ESV). Thank you, Lord, for Your eternal love and guidance and for giving us a plan of goodness we can live by forever. As we learn to surrender our plans to Yours, may You be given all the praise and glory, for it all belongs to You. Amen.

INTRODUCTION

*Be*fore

||||||||||||||||||||||||||

I jumped into an Uber recently and noticed a small sign dangling from the rearview mirror, which read, "Jesus is my Co-Pilot" and, although I was pleased to learn of my driver's good intentions regarding our Savior, I couldn't help but think of how that statement veers off course, theologically speaking. It was a fitting example of how the believing world at large thinks these days that Jesus is here to serve and assist us while we drive and He rides shotgun. Jesus Christ is no one's Co-Pilot. He is *the* Pilot. Another popular phrase made into an even more popular song by Carrie Underwood, "Jesus, Take the Wheel," slides closer to the truth, because it rightly calls for our surrender to Him as the Driver. I wish someone would write a song called "Jesus *Is* the Driver"!

But the truth of needing to place Jesus first doesn't sell many books or garner a mass of likes on social media lately. You can't sell others on living their best life now if you have to first convince them that they're helpless and only God can save them, which is a stark reality our society has conveniently sidestepped. Many with a platform are trying to amass popularity and an increased following by omitting the truth that Jesus is *the Way*. Jesus Himself said it, in John 14:6 (NKJV): "I am the way, the truth, and the life. No one comes to the Father except through Me." Thankfully, there are many still out there who preach this and then give the proper guidance on how to place faith and trust in Him in our daily walk. Likewise, this is the intention of *Plan Be*.

One key reality of placing Christ first is that His ways are opposite of the world's ways. In God's Kingdom, the humble are exalted, the poor are rich, and those who lose themselves in service to Christ will find themselves, precisely because they are not looking to be exalted, rich, or found. For many, this can be a hard pill to swallow. Millions of people throughout the ages have experienced childhoods fraught with neglect or worse, total abandonment by those who should have been there to protect them. Many believe the only way out of a cycle of generational brokenness is to try and fix themselves. Their intentions are noble and I applaud anyone who stands up to fight for a better life. But what they and everyone else needs is for the real, active, engaged, and loving Creator of everything that is—seen and unseen—to be the One we pursue.

In God's economy, to discover we must surrender. We cannot cling to human reason or intellect—we have to let go of what we think we know. We have to learn the delicate dance of stewardship over ownership and releasing what we feel entitled to. That way, if what we release returns, it returns out of freedom, not obligation. We need to hold firmly to belief in God and His goodness, and loosely to everything else. And this belief, or faith, cannot be taken by force—it has to be received as a gift.

The world, ignorant of God, cries, "Go take it! You've earned it!" while the Kingdom of God, abounding in grace, cries, "Simply and humbly receive, without pretense, without status." Everything on this planet is temporal, yet God is eternal. If we can lose ourselves in pursuit of Him, we will find the eternal life we were looking for. Jesus said, "For whoever desires to save his life will lose it, but whoever loses his life for My sake will find it. For what profit is it to a man if he gains the whole world, and loses his own soul? Or what will a man give in exchange for his soul?" (Matthew 16:25–26, NKJV)

A.W. Tozer put it this way: "The meek man cares not at all who is greater than he, for he has long ago decided that the esteem of the world is not worth the effort."

Plan Be is not a feel-good theology to tickle our ears and give us warm fuzzies that God will, as a divine vendor, Amazon Prime to us our deepest wants and pleasures. It is not a book in which we can find ourselves through self-analysis, as if the words contain a magical key that will unlock the door that a thousand other books couldn't.

The goal of *Plan Be* is to shift from heavy introspection and focus on self to a focus on God and discovering His plan for serving Him and others. After all, that's why we're here on this earth: to love and serve God and care for others, and to express His love in our actions toward those in need.

We are to live as light from the light of our Creator and to shine hope and positivity on others by way of love, care, and compassion. We live in a hurting world, and it needs the body of Christ to lift it from the ditch, dress its wounds, and help it heal. As Christ-followers, we're the ones assigned to do this. We have not been assigned to draw inward and practice religious narcissism.

xxii | PLAN BE

The prophet Jeremiah wrote, "This is what the LORD says: 'Don't let the wise boast in their wisdom, or the powerful boast in their power, or the rich boast in their riches. But those who boast should boast in this alone: *that they truly know Me* and understand that I am the LORD who demonstrates unfailing love and who brings justice and righteousness to the earth and that I delight in these things. I, the LORD, have spoken!'" (Jeremiah 9:23–24, NLT, emphasis mine).

I pray that we'll learn to truly know the Lord and, if we are willing, put ourselves aside and engage in this different plan. This is a plan to discover what happens when we search for God, with no thought of ourselves but simply the desire to ride with Him as He drives. This is what *Plan Be* is about, which, as it turns out, is an adventure! God just pulled up to the curb, honking the horn. As we bolt outside to see what's up, He reaches over, swings the passenger-side door open, and shouts, "C'mon, let's go!" That's the life He wants us to experience. He doesn't want us to run back inside and bolt the door.

So, hop in the car, join Him, and ride shotgun! *Plan Be* awaits!

HOW TO *BE*NEFIT FROM THIS BOOK

Plan Be was created to be a quiet time companion, with the principles in this book intended to serve as a roadmap for daily devotion to God. The book portion of *Plan Be* provides the background and context for what I've developed over the years through my own journaling to help maintain a consistent and distraction-free quiet time with God. It includes seven spiritual principles, or "Be-Attitudes," to serve as guidelines for becoming more intimate with Jesus and staying centered and focused on Him. At the end of the book, you'll find a journal template that can be used to guide you daily in the practice of the Be-Attitudes.

Perhaps you're like me, always contending with a racing mind that is hard to slow down or control. As I tried to settle in each morning with the Lord, I was inevitably greeted by a flood of tasks and troubles and any attempt to spend time with Him was assaulted by the concerns of the day. They quickly turned time with Him into a one-way street paved with petitions and complaints as I succumbed to the assault, hurling issues at Him. Communion with God was fraught with continual stops and starts and a distracted, fragmented botchery of half prayers and glossing over the Scriptures. I needed a consistent plan to help dissipate this internal noise and to successfully enter and stay in fellowship with Him.

Simply trying to meditate never worked for this chatty mind, and over the years I learned the most effective means to deal with this was to think through my pen, transferring thoughts from brain to hand onto journal pages. Writing helped me process and provided direction like a trail map does for a trekker or a canvas does for an artist. Journaling has always been beneficial in collecting and making sense of all the random musings, but it wasn't helping shift from self to worship, from problems to praise. The focus was habitually inward. It felt like a constant shaking of the spiritual vending machine, trying to get something out for myself. I desperately wanted to change that, to move from self to a spirit of service. After all, what's the point in all this if it doesn't equip me to love others with the love of Christ?

And that's how the Be-Attitudes were born—to help cultivate the behaviors that would set me up for success in fellowship with and service to Him. There are seven:

The first Be-Attitude, **Breathe,** came about as a means for literally waking up to enter a time with God alert and ready, versus sluggish and slow. It's the "ready, set" before our "go," like an athlete warming up before the race. *Breathe* is a short exercise to clear the fog, or what I call the "mental morning mist." To use a sports analogy, my good friend Cole Campbell refers to this as a "pre-swing routine," taking a few chops with the lumber before stepping into the batter's box, or a few swings with a driver before addressing the golf ball on the tee. I first discovered deep breathing to start the day through a yoga class and found it not only helpful in clearing out the cobwebs and mental clutter, but in experiencing a calming effect. It turned out to be a perfect way to settle into a quiet time awakened and alert (or, to fit Cole's word picture, ready to step up to the plate).

In *Plan Be*, I'll provide deep breathing exercises to help start your quiet time with the Lord. It only takes a minute, but the benefits are long-lasting and can be used not just as you wake but throughout your day, to re-center and enable calm.

The second Be-Attitude is *Be* **Still**. Psalm 46:10 states, "Be still, and know that I am God." It is right that we should come before Him at ease and in a restful state, not frantic or upset. As the breathing exercises help calm us, we can more easily slide into a quiet time with our Savior. To *Be* Still is to "let go." If there's anything still weighing heavy on our minds, we can cast it down, let it fall, drop it, give it to God . . . because He is willing and able to bear our burdens and He cares deeply about our troubles: "Cast your anxieties on Him, because He cares for you" (1 Peter 5:7, ESV). Then we'll be ready to listen in solitude with Him. And then we'll *know* God. We'll become intimate with the great I AM.

The third Be-Attitude is *Be* **Loved**. God calls us "His beloved." The entire Bible is a love letter of redemption in Christ Jesus, of the sacrifice He made to save us because of His great love for us. *Plan Be* will highlight various scriptures to help remind us of the reality of His deep, unending, and unconditional love for us.

The fourth Be-Attitude is ***Beam***, to receive the light of Christ and allow it to work in us and through us. Jesus Christ, who is "the light of the world" (John 8:12, NKJV), also calls us "the light of the world" (Matthew 5:13–16, NKJV). In *Plan Be,* we will enter a time of receiving God's light. We will focus on three actions as we allow His light to shine in our hearts:

- Repent: exposing and confessing our bad thoughts and actions (and ensuing shame and guilt) often hidden in the dark recesses of our hearts.

- Release: laying bare all our hurts and pains; the anger, bitterness, and other negative emotions of being wronged by others.
- Renew: As Ephesians 4:23, NKJV states—to be renewed in the spirit of our minds.

Once we repent and release, then the light of Christ renews us, so that our light can shine before men in such a way that they may see our good works and glorify our Father who is in heaven (Matthew 5:14–16, NKJV). This is where the shift truly happens, from the internal work in which Christ helps renew us to a place where we can begin to focus on serving Him and others.

As renewal happens in our hearts through the *Be*am Be-Attitude, we'll shift to the fifth Be-Attitude, ***Believe***, strengthening our faith through the reading and study of Scripture. What is the Christian life but a trust walk? "Do you believe in Me?" is the question we're continually faced with on our spiritual journey with Christ. And where does faith come by? "Faith comes by hearing, and hearing by the word of God" (Romans 10:17, NKJV). God's Word strengthens our faith and fuels us for the trust walk of life.

The sixth Be-Attitude is ***Be* Joyful**. First Thessalonians 5:16–18 (NIV) encourages us to "rejoice always, pray continually, give thanks in all circumstances; for this is God's will for you in Christ Jesus." In this Be-Attitude, we'll have space to recall joyful moments, pray specifically, and give thanks for His many blessings. This is where the power of journaling comes in, to look back over time on the pages filled with our thoughts, prayers, and thanksgiving, and see God's hand at work in our lives and the lives of those around us.

The seventh and final Be-Attitude is ***Behold***. Time spent in the other Be-Attitudes will prepare our hearts to see God in every moment as we launch into our day and live with a sense of wonder and anticipation of seeing Him at work through us and around us as we serve. *Plan Be* will provide space for journaling these moments of divine noticing and will cultivate a spirit of adventure and expectation as we live knowing God is always at work in every circumstance.

To me, one of the most encouraging verses in Scripture is Galatians 5:1 (GNBDC): "Freedom is what we have—Christ has set us free! Stand firm, then, as free people, and do not allow yourselves to become slaves again." If we practice the Be-Attitudes yet allow ourselves to become shackled again by all that Christ set us free of, then our walk will be hindered, and we'll struggle to live with peace and joy. Each Be-Attitude is coupled with a word to remind us of the freedom and liberty we have, and to serve as a call to action as we apply the concepts to our journeys (we'll expound a little more on Liberties in Chapter 2).

|||||||||||||||||||||||||||||||||||||||||||||||||||||||||||||||||||||||||||||||||||||||||||||||||||||||||

"What light is to the eyes—
What air is to the lungs—
What love is to the heart,
Liberty is to the soul of man."
~ Robert G. Ingersoll, American lawyer, and writer

|||||||||||||||||||||||||||||||||||||||||||||||||||||||||||||||||||||||||||||||||||||||||||||||||||||||||

We are "called to liberty . . . and through love to serve one another" (Galatians 5:13, NKJV). Here are the Liberties, highlighted in bold below:

As we Breathe, we learn to truly **LIVE**.
As we practice how to Be Still before God, we learn to **LET GO**.

As we acknowledge that we are God's Beloved,
we learn how to **LOVE** others.
As we receive the light of Christ in the Beam Be-Attitude,
He will shine His **LIGHT** on others.
As Scripture reinforces that we believe in Him,
we **LEARN** more about Him and learn to walk in His ways.
Practicing how to Be Joyful will cultivate a life of contentment
and we will inevitably **LAUGH** more.
And as we Behold Him,
we learn how to **LOOK** for His presence
and activity in all things.

Authentically living, letting go, loving, shining our light, learning from Him, cultivating a spirit of laughter, and desiring to look to Him with anticipation—these are the freedoms God calls us to as we meditate on the Be-Attitudes.

At the end of each chapter, I have included spaces for responses and journaling as you meditate on what you have read and ask God how your reading should be applied. There, you'll also find your *Be*acon, which is meant to navigate you directly to the very basics of how to practice each Be-Attitude.

At the very end of this book, you'll also find a *Plan Be Be*acon summarizing every Be-Attitude on one page. Feel free to skip to these pages before you begin the book, to acclimate yourself to what *Plan Be* is all about.

I pray these Be-Attitudes will lead your life to a closer walk with God, a life filled with the joy of the Lord, and a heart that longs to serve others!

CHAPTER 1

*Be*coming

||||||||||||||||||||||||

"Before the Lord wills me to do anything,
He first of all wills me to 'be.'
What I do must depend on who I am."
~ Thomas Merton

The year was 2009. Having survived the economic downturn of 2008, I carried on with renewed confidence to my seventeenth year at a global tech company, leading my project management team. Over the previous decade, layoffs at this company had been commonplace, and I was hoping for a quiet year after the hard-hitting one I'd just narrowly escaped. Unfortunately, although this proved to be a better year than the one prior, the axe still fell. Although it felt like a hurricane had passed through in 2008, I was enjoying relative calm in 2009. I was wrong to think it was over.

Turns out, most of 2009 was just the eye of the storm, and the back end of it hit on a Monday in early December, on a day I already dreaded because I had been instructed to lay off two of my employees. It ended up being my day as well. After nearly two decades and over three thousand days of grinding it out at the same employer, I was informed that, in so many words, the company no longer required my knowledge, experience, or time.

That company, which no longer included me in their plans, was at that time my *only* plan. My one plan was to ride that train straight into retirement, or whatever I decided would be in the next phase of my life. This company was my Plan A . . . as well as Plans B, C, D, and E. On that fateful day in December, the company confiscated my travel pass and booted me off the train. Now, suddenly, I was faced with having to entirely reconstruct Plan A.

Would I pursue a similar job at another company? Have to settle for a lesser job elsewhere? Would I blow it all up and change careers? Whatever my choice, I would be starting over. I spent many hours contemplating this, but one thing I did not need to contemplate was that, whichever path I chose, it was vital that I also create a backup plan—a legitimate Plan B—going forward. Never again would I be caught flat-footed by the lack of employment options and alternatives should my number come up again at the next company. With a Plan B, I'd be better able to pivot and shift gears.

In the following months of job (and soul) searching, something profoundly deep was happening within me, something that ended up becoming paramount to the future direction of my life. I pressed into God during this time of job separation, asking Him (and sometimes shouting) questions like:

"*Why did this happen to me?*"

"*Was that whole experience meaningless, wasted?!*"

"What should I do next?"
"Lord, what am I meant to do?"
"What's the plan?!"

. . . and continually praying for my purpose in life to be revealed, because, in my eyes, this career wasn't it.

In waiting for some revelation or direction, "Trust Me" was the answer God continually laid on my spirit, to the point that every morning I'd hear one particular question resonating from Him in my heart: "Do you trust Me?!" At first, realizing I was at the end of my rope, I'd reply with something like this (and admittedly, sometimes in a bitter tone): "I'd better, in lieu of any other options!" But as God continued to heal my broken heart and bruised ego, I started waking up every morning reciting a preemptive response, declaring, "Lord, I trust you." Gradually, those words became my mantra, and eventually, through His graceful work, my core belief.

God came through, as He always does. I learned that God really meant what He said in Proverbs 3:5–6 (ESV): "Trust in the LORD with all your heart and do not lean on your own understanding. In all your ways acknowledge Him, and He will make straight your paths." From a human perspective, I couldn't possibly understand all that was going on; I couldn't answer all the questions. But I learned that God knows all the answers, God cares, and He will make a way.

I gradually learned what Pastor David Jeremiah meant when he said, "There is nothing God doesn't know about your life. You may know the past and present, but God also knows the future. Choose today to walk securely, not in what you know, but in what you believe." Not in what you know, *but in what you believe.*

Be Careful Where You Place Your Trust

My time of unemployment, or what outplacement firms kindly refer to as "transition," was a profound reminder to me of where—and in whom—I should place my trust. Without even realizing it, I'd been placing my trust in what I thought were my abilities, my knowledge, and then trusting in the hands of people who would not—and could not—be responsible for my life. They may have been the overseers of one small aspect of it (i.e., my job), but certainly not the whole. I realized quite painfully that even in that one small compartment of my existence, even they had very little control, being subject as well to the workings of the complex machinery that runs corporations.

This is typically how it goes: somewhere up high in the organization, a report is shared that indicates the company is hemorrhaging profusely, revenue-wise. To stop the bleeding and stave off the loss, someone comes up with a number—cut 10 percent or two million dollars. Salaries are the biggest chunk of dollars, and unfortunately in many cases, the lowest-hanging fruit.

After that, it becomes a list of names. The list may be influenced by many factors chosen over performance, some of which are absolutely real, yet ones that companies would never admit to: salary level, age, tenure, race, religion, and even things like egos at play, petty grievances, or a combination of the above and more. Or perhaps a buyout occurs, and an entire division gets replaced because the new parent has their own personnel. I know of one company that is "trimming the fat" as they prepare to go public with an IPO. If you've ever been a victim of these processes in the corporate world and suddenly been "let go" (as if they were holding on to you, and not the other way around!), then you know how futile it is to trust in man. Certainly, "man" didn't care that I was laid off in December, right before Christmas and at the time of year when no one was hiring, or that I was about to send my first child to college.

Allow me to state who does care: The Lord, who proclaims:

> *"Blessed is the man who trusts in the Lord, and whose hope is the Lord. For he shall be like a tree planted by the waters, which spreads out its roots by the river, and will not fear when heat comes; but its leaf will be green, and will not be anxious in the year of drought, nor will cease from yielding fruit."* (Jeremiah 17:7–8, NKJV)

Hosea had the same picture in mind: "Let us know; let us press on the know the Lord; His going out is sure as the dawn; He will come to us as showers, as the spring rains that water the earth" (Hosea 6:3, ESV).

I felt nourished and replenished as I pressed into God, as I earnestly sought Him and relied on Him. Where I could've drowned in the deluge of the world's monsoon, instead I felt the healing shower of His refreshing rain—His living water—falling on me. God is reliable! He's completely unfazed by our daunting circumstances. He's bigger than all of them and He keeps His promises to care for us and guide us through it all. To simply believe Him in that is our part. "For I am about to do something new. See, I have already begun! Do you not see it? I will make a pathway through the wilderness. I will create rivers in the dry wasteland" (Isaiah 43:19, NLT).

What we see as an end, God sees as a beginning. Where we see a desert and no clear means of travel, He creates rivers there for us to ride upon. He turns impossible situations into possible ones.

Before the encouragement we read in Jeremiah 17—that those who hope and trust in the Lord would be blessed—God provides a warning in verses 5 and 6 (CEB): "Cursed are those who trust in mere humans, who depend on human strength and turn their hearts from the LORD. They will be like a desert shrub that doesn't know when relief comes. They will live in the parched places of the wilderness, in a barren land where no one survives."

I can certainly testify that trusting in mere humans does not make for a viable Plan A! Trusting in mortals rather than God brings on stress and fear, and ultimately, treachery and misfortune. It is a dry and barren place. According to Jeremiah, when we place our trust in God we are like a towering tree with strong roots. Our trunks grow strong and high and our branches reach up and out in harmony with the deep strength of our roots. But when we place our trust in man, we're merely a shrub. Our growth is stunted; we're just twigs with leaves, a surface-level root system crawling with thirst. Trusting in God brings on vitality, life, hope, and good results, even in times of drought. By trusting in God, good fruit will result. We don't bear fruit, He does.

Jesus said, "Remain united to me, and I will remain united to you. A branch cannot bear fruit by itself; it can do so only if it remains in the vine. In the same way, you cannot bear fruit unless you remain in Me. I am the vine, and you are the branches. Those who remain in Me, and I in them, will bear much fruit; for you can do nothing without Me" (John 15:4–5, GNBDC).

We are the branch; He is the Vine. He produces the fruit as we stay connected to Him. And I learned, through what would normally be a miserable experience, that staying connected to Him was far easier than trying to produce fruit on my own.

This is a beautiful thing! Why? Because "My Father's glory is shown by your bearing much fruit, and in this way you become my disciples. I love you just as the Father loves me; remain in my love" (John 15:8–9, GNBDC). When we trust in Him, remain in His love, and *allow Him to work through us* (versus us trying to create and force our way upon Him), the fruit will result in glorifying God. And that's what life is all about—bringing glory to our Creator as He draws others to Himself through our experiences.

I should pause to make a point here regarding trust: certainly, there are people in our lives who are trustworthy. However, that will be a very small circle. And even those we deem trustworthy aren't perfect. Mistakes can be made, even from those we entrust our hearts to. No one is perfect, only Christ is. Our trust in Him must be first and foremost, above all. We must rely on the God of Psalm 111:7 (ESV): "The works of His hands are faithful and just; all His precepts are trustworthy."

As we read back through the Jeremiah verses in chapter 17 in context, it speaks of those who turn their hearts from the Lord because, instead, they choose to trust in human strength. There are a few people in my life whom I trust, but this trust is a mutual trust cultivated by intimacy and born first in my heart from the foundation—the root system of an intimate relationship with God. Trust God first, and through the power of the Holy Spirit, He will teach you how and whom to trust at the human level.

He Is Greater than I

When self is god, though, we do the work. We sweat and toil and strive. We stress and find little as we repeat this tumultuous cycle daily. However, when Christ is Lord, He does the work. When we take His yoke (an instrument of labor) upon us, the work is easy and the burden is light. And we find rest for our souls:

> *"Come to Me, all who labor and are heavy*
> *laden, and I will give you rest. Take My yoke*
> *upon you, and learn from Me, for I am gentle*
> *and lowly in heart, and you will find rest*
> *for your souls. For my yoke is easy, and my*
> *burden is light." (Matthew 11:28–30, ESV)*

Are you trusting in God? Really trusting in Him? As I write this, I'm faced with another daunting employment situation. I hinted at it above when I mentioned a buyout. But I'm not worried. I've played this game before. Not my first rodeo, and certainly not God's! I've learned that God always comes through. He is reliable, and He is the One who is in control. "'I am the Alpha and the Omega,' says the Lord God, 'who is and who was and who is to come, the Almighty'" (Revelation 1:8, ESV). It is time to come and place our complete trust in the One who is the first of all things, the last of all things, and in all things: "And those who know Your name will put their trust in You; For You, LORD, have not forsaken those who seek you" (Psalm 9:10, NKJV).

God will always be with you. He will never leave you. That's a promise! Not only that, but He will give you peace only He can give as you trust Him. He proved this to me and what Isaiah 26:3 (ESV) says resonates deeply in my experience: "You will keep in perfect peace, whose mind is stayed on You because he trusts in You."

The translation of the word "stayed" is to "place or lay something upon anything, so that it may rest upon, and be supported by it."[1] Trust in God and allow your mind to rest upon and be supported by Him as you do, and you will receive His peace, or

---

1   [Gesenius's Hebrew-Chaldee Lexicon for H5564—*camak*, stayed] Wilhelm, Gesenius Friedrich Heinrich, and Samuel Prideaux Tregelles. *Genesius's Hebrew and Chaldee Lexicon to the Old Testament Scriptures.* London: Bagster, 1846.

His *shalom*—all-encompassing and complete soundness, welfare, tranquility, and contentment.

And I know there is no one, no God more powerful than the One I serve: "You are great and powerful, glorious, splendid, and majestic. Everything in heaven and earth is yours, and you are king, supreme ruler over all" (1 Chronicles 29:11, GNBDC). God always comes through! Lean on Him, pursue Him, and get close to Him in prayer and in His Word. He will not forsake you, regardless of the situations you face. I am a personal witness to the fact that He will guide you to a victorious path! And in this process of walking through the valley, of struggling through the test—I came to learn that this journey was less about what I should do next in my career and more about who I needed to become in my character.

What I thought would be an outside job was actually an inside job. You see, Jesus sees it all. We create all these appearances for ourselves that might look good on the outside. We work hard to curate a certain image and control how the world sees us. But the thing is, Jesus isn't interested in appearances. He works on us from the heart, from the inner depths of who we are deep within our character. I had the appearance of strong faith, but in reality, it was fragile, hanging by a thread! It took a crisis moment for me to realize this. If you're a professing Christian, He simply will not allow your character to reflect anyone else's but His own. And He will spend your entire lifetime refining it so that, from the inside out, you show the observing world that you are a legitimate son or daughter of the King.

Jesus Is the Pilot

Eventually, the "What should I do?" question was answered, but more importantly, God guided me to answer the question I didn't even know I had at first: "Who should I be?" God altered my perspective as I looked for a Plan B. In its place, He showed me a *Plan Be*—growth in character as I laid my own agenda aside and learned how to surrender to Him. The principles of life He taught me during this time, and in the decade following it, would become the foundation for this work and for the journal I'd develop to help keep me on His path.

In God's realm, *Plan Be* comes before Plan A. Whether you're facing job loss (or loss of any kind), no matter what hardship or struggle you're up against, I believe wholeheartedly that the following principles—or as I like to call them, Be-Attitudes—if attended to every day, will help in growing you as a person and more importantly, in your intimacy with God. He is far more interested in making a significant impact in the development of your heart, soul, mind, and spirit than in accomplishing whatever tasks you take on, whatever earthly goals you create, or whatever performance objectives you strive for. A strong tree has deep roots, and drawing close to God is like being close to life-giving waters. God alone will develop our root system and keep us well-watered and refreshed so that we may stand tall in seasons of drought, heat, or any adversity that comes our way.

God wasn't going to settle for me (and He won't settle for you either) to do anything for Him without seriously and thoroughly developing our character. What we're truly meant to do must come from who we are as maturing persons of faith, virtue, and character, in relationship to Him. If what we do does not come out of authenticity—of who we truly are at our core—then we'll never be at peace with our life, let alone our vocation. However, when we find God, we find everything.

Most of us have forgotten how to *be*. We, especially Americans, first strive to *do*. Job number one is performance, sales, and results. And in doing so, most of us (if we admit it) are left unfulfilled, even while we're successful (as the world measures success). We get the gold, but we burn out in the process. We trade time for money, slaving away to buy more things, somehow convincing ourselves that the trophies we surround ourselves with will somehow sustain our satisfaction. We climb the ladder, striving to show in our circles that we're living the dream. We post it, we tweet it, and we snap it, but quickly those images fade; the façade blurs and we're left once again facing the reality that stares back at us from the mirror.

God's will for us, though, is not performance or position, but to become people of character. It's a mystery, but what He develops in us has eternal implications, something significant that extends far beyond the days we spend here on Earth. Vocation matters, but the person behind that vocation matters more; and in that, God develops us not so we get things done, but so we become. Vocation is simply another tool in the hands of our eternal Potter as He shapes us, the delicate jars of clay we are. The change He works in us is not to perform better and multiply our results, but rather to improve our character—our heart, our compassion, kindness, grace, goodness, peace, patience, gentleness, self-control, hope, and ultimately our love. Many of these God calls the "fruits of the Spirit" (Galatians 5:22–23), the result of what the Holy Spirit works in us. They are not called the "Fruits of Denny" or the "Fruits of <insert your name here>." Jesus says, "I am the vine; you are the branches. If you remain in me and I in you, you will bear much fruit; apart from me you can do nothing" (John 15:5, NIV).

Now that's a very definitive statement—that apart from Him we can do nothing. Zilch. Zero. As Christ-followers, as branches that remain in Him, the Vine, we will all get tutored in that lesson eventually. It's a lesson we all must learn. The branches do not make the fruit: they simply receive it. In the area of my life where I thought I was in control, where I had invested the most effort—my blood, sweat, and tears through decades of work in my profession—God showed me who really was in control and that apart from Him I could do nothing. I was too stubborn to get out of my own way and give rightful honor to the One who deserves first place—God. My striving never served the branch; it simply withered. Our efforts dry up, but in following Jesus we get the vine, the supply, and the result is fruit because of what He can do as we abide.

That was lesson number one: I'm not in control. Man is not in control. God is. Lesson number two was that, in giving up control and sincerely handing my life over to Him, I needed to stop making requests of Him about what I wanted Him to do and how I wanted Him to do it. An "I love God as long as He blesses me" faith is not true faith. That's Aladdin faith. True faith is believing in God and surrendering the outcomes to Him. For lesson number two, it's as if I was saying, "Sure God, take the wheel, but I'm going to tell you where I'm going. You drive, I'll navigate." But God doesn't need your map. He knows perfectly well where He's going with you.

Living by Faith

Admittedly, this is a very hard lesson to learn, one that I'm still learning, honestly. I want the path of least resistance. I want an easy ride. And I want everything I want along the way, no waiting. I want to arrive at the destination of my choosing. It's like placing faith in myself and asking God to make things happen. But what is faith? Hebrews 11:1 (ESV) says that "faith is the assurance of things hoped for, the conviction of things not seen." The biblical definition of "hope" is essentially a confident expectation of good. Biblical hope is not wishing upon a star to maybe get what we want. Biblical hope is the absolute knowing that what God has promised already has happened or will happen. And the things He makes happen are ultimately for our good, whether we experience them in this life or the life ever after. Hence, the "conviction of things not seen."

We have to believe that although we don't see it all, He does, and because He does, He knows exactly what's going on and He understands the purposes for which they occur. Just because I don't like what's going on in my life or the lives around me doesn't mean there isn't a purpose in it. Scripture says that "We know that all things work together for the good of those who love God, who are called according to his purpose" (Romans 8:28, CSB). What this verse doesn't say is that everything always works in our favor. Of course, it doesn't. But God, in His unmatchable, infinite wisdom, knows how to work all things for good. He is *good*. It takes faith and hope to not only understand that but to try and live it out every day, especially when the outcomes we're experiencing are less than what we'd deem favorable.

Take the apostle Paul, for example. In Hebrews 12, he doesn't encourage us to fix our eyes on the goal or finish line. For the Christian, the finish line is ours already (eternity with the Trinity in heaven)! We are, rather, encouraged to fix our eyes upon a person—Jesus Christ. In Him, we can run with determination the race set before us. He is the Author and Finisher of what is vital in our lives—faith. Remember my question from God: "Do you trust Me?" His Son Jesus Christ did not give up! He focused on the joy set before Him (see Hebrews 12:2). His prize was not a trophy. It was spending eternity with God and the reality of bringing us with Him. His joy is us, joy in human lives. It was the promise of healing our character, attitude, hearts, souls, and joy that motivated Him to persevere through pain and pass the ultimate test of faith.

And so we persevere on our journey, learning how to set aside our own Plan A and trusting Him to work out His plans for our life—Plan Be—and we learn that:

In Plan A, our results determine our attitude.
In *Plan Be*, our attitude determines our results.

In Plan A, action precedes faith.
In *Plan Be*, faith precedes action.

In Plan A, it's performance over people.
In *Plan Be*, it's people over performance.

In Plan A, we work for the acceptance of man.
In *Plan Be*, we work *from* acceptance of God.

Belief Is Freedom

Paul and Silas were in prison, deep within the dungeon, feet fastened to the stocks. It was midnight—the darkest hour—and yet there they were, praying and singing hymns to God. Suddenly an earthquake hit, shaking the doors open and unfastening the chains that shackled every prisoner. Assuming the prisoners had escaped, the jailer drew his sword that he might take his own life (knowing he would've had his life taken from him, being that he was responsible for the prisoners). But Paul cried out to the jailer in a loud voice to say they were all still there.

The jailer called for a light, sprang in, and fell trembling before Paul and Silas, pleading, "Sirs, what must I do to be saved?" Paul replied, 'Believe in the Lord Jesus, and you will be saved.'" (See Acts 16:30–31.)

Paul and Silas didn't respond to the jailer with a list of actions to take, or with a deceptive plot or alibi to enact. They didn't throw the Ten Commandments at him or recite Levitical law with a set of conditions he must meet first; they didn't assign him a curriculum to follow or a test to pass. The only requirement was that he believe in the Lord Jesus.

When it comes to salvation, God may go to great lengths to get someone's attention, and He may go to great lengths to involve us in the process. However, the decision of one being saved requires no more than a simple step of faith. It's not meant to be hard.

Elsewhere Paul tells us: "For it is by believing in your heart that you are made right with God, and it is by openly declaring your faith that you are saved" (Romans 10:10, NLT). We aren't made right in God's eyes by checking off a list of rules.

Also, we can't overlook this point: when you read of them singing hymns to God . . . *while in prison!* . . . you get the impression that they were not dwelling on their own circumstances, feeling sorry for themselves. Certainly, they weren't belting out woe-is-me songs. They were focused not on themselves but on God. That's the whole emphasis behind *Plan Be*—focus on and trust in God.

But the radically simple act of believing doesn't just provide the gift of salvation. We are to continually live in this simplicity of faith with the same effortless wonder that brought us to and through His saving grace. It has taken me so long to get this. This used to be my banner: "The Lord made me free. Beyond that, it's all up to me."

But what if He meant for our entire lives to be free, void of striving? And what if He offers ongoing freedom as much as He does the gift of salvation? Doesn't it say in Galatians 5:1

(GNBDC), "Freedom is what we have—Christ has set us free!
Stand, then, as free people, and do not allow yourselves to become
slaves again"? He set us free so that we could *continue* to be free,
unshackled from legalism and stifling world systems, and living in
boundless joy as He directs our lives. He didn't save us to imprison
us with more rules and regulations and what they ultimately lead
to—performance expectations.

We cannot work our way into salvation. He does the saving.
We simply need to believe. This is called faith—a trust in the One
who can save our souls.

What Shall We Do?

The crowds were following Jesus and caught up with Him in
Capernaum, having pursued Him from the other side of the sea.
They were intent on receiving an answer to this question: "What
shall we do, so that we may work the works of God?" Did Jesus
start rattling off a list of things they must do? No, His answer was
beautifully simple. He said to them, "This is the work of God, that
you believe in Him whom He has sent" (John 6:28–29, NASB).
That's it? Just . . . believe? Yes! That's the simple, powerful good
news of Jesus Christ!

But, you ask, what about our actions, our works? Doesn't the
Bible say, "Faith without works is dead" (James 2:17, NKJV, para-
phrased)? Don't our works prove our faith? Yes, but works will
flow from faith naturally. Consider this from MacLaren's exposition on Ephesians 2:10: "To work up toward salvation is, in the
strict sense of the words, preposterous; it is inverting the order of
things. It is beginning at the wrong end. It is saying X Y Z before
you have learned to say A B C. We are to work downward from
salvation because we have it, not that we may get it." You can't
work your way into believing in God or perform your way into

earning His acceptance. In following this thought and in the context of *Plan Be*, being comes before doing; yet most of us, around the swirling influence of the world, focus on the doing. And this *doing* is so insidious that if we're not careful, it will take over even our most sacred institutions.

For the Christian, belief is huge. In fact, it's everything. Jesus asked this question in several scenes—"Do you believe that I am able to do this?" (Matthew 9:28, ESV). He stated, "Repent and believe in the gospel" (Mark 1:15, ESV), and encouraged those around Him by saying, "All things are possible to him who believes" (Mark 9:23, ESV), and "Whatever you ask in prayer, believe that you have received it, and it will be yours" (Mark 11:24, ESV).

This is truly liberating! Much anxiety in the world today comes from performance, specifically from a perceived lack of it (usually from others, but we also can be our own worst critics). We're told that results will get us what we want and make us happy. And when we fall short—whether, in our own eyes or the eyes of others, we experience stress, depression, anger, frustration, and a potential myriad of other negative emotions. But God gives us freedom first, not freedom last! Freedom isn't something we're to attain at the end of our days; it's ours right now, in the present moment, and forever! Life was not meant to be a continuous escape attempt from Alcatraz; it was meant to be free of the chains and shackles of the world's systems so that we can truly live free.

CHAPTER 2

The *Be*-Attitudes

IIIIIIIIIIIIIIIIIIIIIIIIII

Contained in the Sermon on the Mount, found in Matthew 5 (and the Sermon on the Plain, found in Luke 6), are what have been referred to as the "Beatitudes," a term that comes from the Latin Vulgate *beati sunt*, or "blessed are"—nine profound declarations, each beginning with these words from what many consider to be Jesus' most profound teaching. His Beatitudes describe the blessedness of those who have certain qualities or experiences unique to those belonging to the kingdom of heaven.[2]

Before this famous sermon, Jesus had spent the entire night up on the mountain, alone with and praying to God. As He descended from it the next morning, He was joined by His twelve disciples and met by a large crowd of other disciples and followers from Judea, Jerusalem, and the coastal cities of Tyre and Sidon.

---

2   "Beatitude." *Encyclopædia Britannica*. Encyclopædia Britannica, Inc., July 20, 1998. https://www.britannica.com/topic/Beatitude-biblical-literature.

Suffice to say it was quite a large crowd, gathered from all over the region. Luke 6:18–19 (CEV) states they had "come to listen to Jesus and to be healed of their diseases. All who were troubled by evil spirits were also healed. Everyone was trying to touch Jesus because power was going out from him and healing them all."

He'd just spent the entire night up on the mountain with God and was undoubtedly empowered in many ways during that time. He climbed up and away from the multitudes for solitude, connection, and a time of communication (that is, prayer) with the Almighty. What came out of that focused time with Him was an equipping so profound that Jesus' body literally could not contain all the blessing and glory, and it overflowed powerfully to anyone who was able to touch Him. This power flowed as well from His mouth as He spoke the life-changing words that turned upside down the notion of who was considered to be truly blessed, or happy.

Certainly, happy are the healed, the rich, the self-sufficient, those victorious in battle, those cared for and (supposedly) without a care in the world, the ones enjoying good fortune and favor, who are continually well fed and full, right?

Not so, according to Jesus. There is such a danger in self-sufficiency because we can tend to forget God and start to believe the lie that all the good things we have and experience are the results of our efforts; we ultimately cultivate a mindset of entitlement, expecting continual pleasure and good fortune to the point that the need for God fades into the background. And it's exponentially more dangerous when, after all that good fortune, we blame our hardships on God when the hardships eventually come around. When, in all the good things, a person begins to become their own god of the world around them, Jesus says they're trading the everlasting blessing of His kingdom for a temporary worldly satisfaction that can never be satiated. Truly happy are the ones who sincerely recognize their need for God and the futility of pursuing happiness apart from Him. This was the profile of the crowd that had gathered around Him. They needed healing, and healing He gave. But He also knew that in short order, many would depart back to their normal lives and face once again the challenges of existing on this planet.

Mountains and Valleys

Christ knows that with every valley there's a summit, but with every summit, there's a valley. Here He was, having just descended from the mountain, having received God's glory, and now facing the throngs of broken and needy people in the valley below (see Luke 6:18–19). So, He healed many and gave them a mountaintop experience, all the while knowing that, humanly speaking, they couldn't stay there.

Life is a sojourn, and it's inevitable that at some point we'll have to come back down from the summit. In the journey, Jesus was conveying that the truly happy ones are those who have the same trust for God in the valleys as they do on the peaks, and those who don't blame God for mishaps and misfortunes after praising Him for the good fortunes and success. God always shows up in good times and bad (actually, He never really leaves the scene, though within our limited perspective we think He does), and He works most profoundly in our pain and difficulties because He is the Healer. He is the Deliverer, the Conqueror.

An intimate relationship with Him involves our ascents and descents, both our summits and our valleys. He is in it all. Of course, He's the source of all good. But Jesus emphasizes in the Beatitudes that He's the God of all those who see themselves and their situations as less than, disadvantaged. We're never promised continual good fortune after we come to Him. He didn't say that "all things will be good" for those who love Him and are called according to His purposes. What He did say is that "all things work together for good to those who love God, to those who are the called according to His purpose" (Romans 8:28, NKJV). All things—good and bad—will work together to result in good things, such as a stronger, more resilient, and refined character.

Adversity, pain, setbacks, job loss, and other struggles have a way of changing us to become more like Christ when we live in a way that knows and leans on God's promise that He has a purpose for us in these experiences. Whether we're just now grabbing the rope of opportunity, or at the end of one with no alternatives in sight, He is there with us. He has experienced the setbacks, adversity, physical and mental anguish—the betrayal, the broken-heartedness, and the impact on body and soul from crushing blows dealt by evildoers—and He is with us.

"When the righteous cry for help, the LORD hears and delivers them out of all their troubles. The LORD is near to the broken-hearted and saves the crushed in spirit. Many are the afflictions of the righteous, but the LORD delivers him out of them all" (Psalm 39:17–19, ESV).

I'm (Not) All Ears

Near the age of forty, I reached the end of my rope. I had contracted a disease of the middle ear known as cholesteatoma, which is the growth of a cyst where the skin cells clump together behind the ear drum. If not treated, the condition can potentially cause permanent hearing loss—or worse, spread to the brain. The way it was described to me was that if you were to open a pumpkin, the webbing inside is much like what was growing inside my inner ears, and in my particular case, both sides. At the same time. And, it was slowly eating away at my middle ear bones—the hammer, anvil, and stirrup.

I've had ear problems all my life—continual infections in both ears, resulting in a dozen or more surgeries (I stopped counting) starting around the age of eight. For thirty-two years, I'd been defending the attacks of hearing loss, and now this.

Imagine you're listening to the radio. The music is at a healthy volume and you're rockin'.

But, unbeknownst to you, someone walks over to the source and turns the volume down half a notch. Then a while later they go back and turn it down again, ever so slightly. At first, you don't notice; you can hear the sound quite well. It's not until a good while after the sound has been continually and very gradually reduced that you begin to discern that something's not quite right. This goes on until you reach a point when you finally realize, *Hey, I'm not hearing that music very well anymore. What happened?*

Cholesteatoma—at least in my experience—was like this, a very subtle, gradual decline in audio recognition over a protracted course of time. At first, I thought the problem was with the source of whatever I was trying to hear. Somebody was turning the volume down. *Why is that person talking so softly? Why is the audio on the TV so muffled? Why are they whispering?*

Gradual hearing loss is very hard to detect by the person experiencing it. For instance, during this time of hearing decline, if you spoke to me while I was looking away, I didn't have a clue that I didn't hear you. I was given feedback from friends who told me that I was frequently being labeled by others as aloof, or even arrogant because I was supposedly ignoring them. Lord knows how many communication attempts I missed during this time. Thankfully, those who knew my past set the record straight for those who didn't, but in many ways, it affected my relationships.

As the volume slowly declined, my family had to gradually speak louder to carry on a conversation with me. They too didn't realize what was going on at first. Not until repeated episodes of them having to restate what they'd said, and having to talk to me at a higher volume, did they realize something was seriously wrong. It reached the point where my wife and kids were understandably getting worn out trying to converse with me. I was starting to feel more alone and isolated.

The cholesteatoma became so bad that I needed to wear hearing aids in both ears. It helped, but the technology back then wasn't very good. Today, hearing aids are Bluetooth compatible! You can control the volume from your smartphone and immediately adjust to the environment. But the kind I had were manual, and digging into each ear to adjust the volume was increasingly aggravating. Plus, I continued to suffer from infections and the resulting drainage kept shorting my hearing aids out. I'd have to take them in for repair, during which time I was reduced to near deafness. By this time, cholesteatoma had eroded more than 70 percent of my hearing in both ears.

I remember visiting many doctors during this dark valley journey. One after another told me there was nothing they could do, except for antibiotics. I perceived that there was more than one doctor who didn't want to touch me with a ten-foot pole, given my history of surgeries. Too risky. Or not worth it. Other doctors were simply perplexed. I stopped seeing them because we'd hit a wall, treatment-wise. "Just keep wearing the hearing aids," they said. "You'll never hear well without them."

I went through two years of this. I wouldn't be exaggerating to say it nearly ruined me. I stopped talking: why put someone through the burden of communicating with me? Consequently, I withdrew from social situations. For someone who loves people and human interaction and values relationships, this condition sent me into depression. I felt like I was in a deep, dark hole with no way out. My deep love for music was severely affected; in a word picture, it was as if someone splattered ink all over the song sheet. I couldn't distinguish the notes. Everything was muffled; everything sounded muddy. In short, I was shut up, shut out, and put out.

What kind of God would allow this to happen? I was teaching Sunday school, for crying out loud. I couldn't hear anyone's prayers. My children were confused. Why isn't Dad talking? I was a manager of people in my job, which I couldn't do very well if I wasn't able to communicate.

Needless to say, I was feeling quite sorry for myself. But it's precisely in these moments where Jesus says, "Here I Am." He is there in those moments when you (and your loved ones) have exhausted all possibilities to remedy the situation, having tried in your own strength to fix the problems to no avail, when you've thrown your hands up and cried out that you're cooked, and cannot see a way out. He says, "Let go of the problem you're holding, and take my hand. Let go of the rope; I've got it."

So I did. I prayed, "Lord, if you can't fix this, then no one can." He heard my cry. One morning at my wife Jill's place of work, they gathered before the store opened to pray, which was the custom there every day. In her desperation, she asked the team to pray for the healing of my ears. That's when a co-worker shared with her about a relative who'd been through a revolutionary surgical procedure after similar difficulties and had been healed. It involved replacing the hammer, anvil, and stirrup with a titanium column in the middle ear. Immediately upon hearing this from Jill, we booked an appointment with an ENT, Dr. Fred Owens, in Dallas. I remember on my first visit, he looked at me and said in his slow Texas drawl, "We'll get you fixed up." For the first time in a very long while, I was filled with hope.

What followed were surgeries on both ears to implant the titanium columns in my middle ear sections and I'm elated to report that to this day, my hearing in both ears has been almost fully restored. I'll always remember the post-op appointment, after the healing process and the confirmation that my hearing was back to normal. I was searching for a way to thank him for his willingness to operate on me and instill hope in my heart, and for the beautiful results that came from his skillful hands. As I sat in the appointment room waiting for him to come in, I stared at a framed picture on the wall of Amen Corner at Augusta National golf course, featuring one of the most iconic and gorgeous golf holes in the world. I'd also noticed in other rooms throughout all of my visits various golf-related pictures. His entire office was dotted with various images of the sport; undoubtedly he had a love for the game. I knew then how to thank him. So, when he came into the room to see me and we shook hands, I looked at him and said, "Dr. Owens, I've been trying to find a suitable way to thank you for all you've done. The best way I can put it, sir, is that you just hit a hole in one on a par five." Since that day, I don't think I've ever seen a smile that wide.

Being a part of this miracle made Jesus' words in the Beatitudes come together in a whole new light.

Jesus' Beatitudes

As conveyed beautifully by Eugene Peterson in his paraphrase *The Message*, here are Jesus' Beatitudes from Matthew 5:3–12. I'm going to include the ESV as well for a more traditional context:

Verse 3:

- ESV: Blessed are the poor in spirit, for theirs is the kingdom of heaven.
- MSG: You're blessed when you're at the end of your rope. With less of you there is more of God and his rule.

Verse 4:

- ESV: Blessed are those who mourn, for they shall be comforted.
- MSG: You're blessed when you feel you've lost what is most dear to you. Only then can you be embraced by the One most dear to you.

Verse 5:

- ESV: Blessed are the meek, for they shall inherit the earth.
- MSG: You're blessed when you're content with just who you are—no more, no less. That's the moment you find yourselves proud owners of everything that can't be bought.

Verse 6:

- ESV: Blessed are those who hunger and thirst for righteousness, for they shall be satisfied.
- MSG: You're blessed when you've worked up a good appetite for God. He's food and drink in the best meal you'll ever eat.

Verse 7:

- ESV: Blessed are the merciful, for they shall receive mercy.
- MSG: You're blessed when you care. At the moment of being "care-full," you find yourselves cared for.

Verse 8:

- ESV: Blessed are the pure in heart, for they shall see God.
- MSG: You're blessed when you get your inside world— your mind and heart—put right. Then you can see God in the outside world.

Verse 9:
- ESV: Blessed are the peacemakers, for they shall be called sons of God.
- MSG: You're blessed when you can show people how to cooperate instead of compete or fight. That's when you discover who you really are, and your place in God's family.

Verse 10:
- ESV: Blessed are those who are persecuted for righteousness' sake, for theirs is the kingdom of heaven.
- MSG: You're blessed when your commitment to God provokes persecution. The persecution drives you even deeper into God's kingdom.

Verse 11:
- ESV: Blessed are you when others revile you and persecute you and utter all kinds of evil against you falsely on my account.
- MSG: Not only that—count yourselves blessed every time people put you down or throw you out or speak lies about you to discredit me. What it means is that the truth is too close for comfort and they are uncomfortable.

Verse 12:
- ESV: Rejoice and be glad, for your reward is great in heaven, for so they persecuted the prophets who were before you.
- MSG: You can be glad when that happens—give a cheer, even!—for though they don't like it, I do! And all heaven applauds. And know that you are in good company. My prophets and witnesses have always gotten into this kind of trouble.

If we just stay connected to Jesus, not only will we get through the dark valleys, we'll shine on the other side. We'll experience a depth of joy we've never experienced before, not a joy borne from ease and favor and relief from being spared from difficulty, but from the conquering, victorious win in battle. There's a satisfaction that runs deeper with overcoming and growth than through charity and skating through the status quo. I believe this is part of what Jesus may have been getting at when He prayed to the Father that those He was given by God not be taken out of the world, but that God would keep them from the Evil One (see John 17:15, NKJV). It goes with His saying earlier in John 16:33 that "In the world, you will have tribulation; but be of good cheer, I have overcome the world." I've come to learn in my Christian walk that God seems to prefer teaching us how to live victoriously *through* hardship rather than merely saving us *from* it. Of course, there are times when He does rescue us from calamity, but more often than not our journey is marked with hills to climb and valleys to push through.

Why is life this way? Here are a couple of reasons: to praise Him and to bless others. Difficulties aren't meant to take us down, they are meant to refine us. Refining is a process of purifying; His desire is to make us pure ("blessed are the pure in heart") and the adversities of life are what are most often used to remove the dross—the imperfections, the soot, and grime—from our souls. And these experiences later serve as anchors when other storms come in. We can look back with confidence knowing that our Savior will come through again, as He always does. And the experiences He gives us should be used to pay it forward, supporting others going through similar valleys.

There's something about the difficulties of life that drives us to find a source beyond what humans can fix. The seeking, the searching, and yes, even the desperation can forge a strength within us that ease and pleasure simply cannot. No one asks for pain and hardship, yet this is an indisputable fact of life—there will be valleys. What I learned in my ear experience, as well in other trials, is the profound joy of knowing, in our inevitable episodes of pain, that God is there not just in the midst of it, but involved in it, engaged, and prepared to lead us through. We are not without hope. Ever. And that's what Jesus conveys in the Beatitudes. You are blessed, ultimately, in adverse circumstances, because God will be there for you and He will see you through it, and you will grow in character as a result and you—child of the kingdom—will draw ever nearer to the King of it.

God Will Always *Be* Faithful

No one knew this better than the apostle Paul. He poured out his life experience and wisdom to a young pastor named Timothy and while he was profoundly encouraging to Timothy, he never sugarcoated what life would be like for those who desire to follow Christ. In his second letter to Timothy, he rather bluntly states: "Yes, and all who desire to live godly in Christ Jesus will suffer persecution" (2 Timothy 3:12, NKJV). But listen to what he tells Timothy just before this: "But you have carefully followed my doctrine, manner of life, purpose, faith, longsuffering, love, perseverance, persecutions, afflictions, which happened to me at Antioch, at Iconium, at Lystra—what persecutions I endured. And out of them *all* the Lord delivered me" (2 Timothy 3:10–11, NKJV, emphasis mine).

Yes, life is hard. But God is faithful and will see us through not some of it, or most of it, but *all* of it!

"Even though I walk through the [sunless] valley of the shadow of death, I fear no evil, for You are with me; Your rod [to protect] and Your staff [to guide], they comfort and console me." (Psalm 23:4, AMP). God's guarantees for His followers are many, but two that are paramount and should give us much peace and confidence is that He is always with us and will always see us *through* our journey in life, especially as we travel through dark valleys.

So, like Jesus' Beatitudes, *Plan Be* is built around the blessings of Being and Attitudes, or Be-Attitudes. These are like pillars to support the structure of our life under the direction of God before self. They are meant to fortify us in all seasons of life: the mountaintop, the valley, and every climb or descent in between, knowing He is with us in every single step. As we focus on the seven Be-Attitudes in *Plan Be* and incorporate them into our lives, we will effectively shift our focus away from trying to operate in our limited strength and instead focus on the true source of life—God. We will live out in every scene what it means to be truly blessed. We will learn to shift from anxiety-riddled, performance-based living to the joy-filled freedom of following the One who directs our lives and shapes our characters.

Jesus' attitude was one of selfless, humble service to His Master, obedient from start to finish. He laid down His majesty and His rights to identify with us as He lived on our level, saving us from impending doom. He made Himself nothing so that we could be given everything, and in doing, so He modeled the example of how we should live for others.

Liberties

With each Be-Attitude in this book is a corresponding freedom. I call these "Liberties" because each Be-Attitude equips us with the freedom, or liberty, to act in accordance with His principles. These Liberties are not forced, but natural and free, completely opposite to the spirits of duty, regulation, or legalism. This, again, is based on the premise of Galatians 5:1 (NKJV): "Stand fast therefore in the liberty by which Christ has made us free, and do not be entangled again with a yoke of bondage."

To "stand fast" is to remain continually, to persevere. We should live our lives in constant freedom as we act, and as we behave toward ourselves and others. In Christ, we are no longer slaves held in bondage by the restrictive systems of the world, which include judgment, entitlement, and a sense of superiority and focus on our needs over the needs of others. Dictionary. com defines freedom as "the power to determine action without restraint," and "exemption from external control, interference, regulation, etc." In Christ we are given the freedom to do His will, to act—based on His principles—without concern for retribution. Under man's control, we experience restriction, dominance, and fear. Under God's control, we experience, grace, love, and freedom.

The Holy Spirit produces fruit in us as we walk in Christ, and against these fruits, as Paul states, "there is no law" (Galatians 5:23, NKJV). They are legal, edifying, holy, and just, and they operate in total freedom. Likewise, the Liberties in *Plan Be* cannot be restricted by man; they are limited only by the limits we place on ourselves. In other words, the Spirit empowers us to choose and use these Liberties without cost or limit. There are no restrictions; we have the freedom to exercise them fully!

In this freedom, we are compelled to act, to do for Him what comes from being, and the Liberties in *Plan Be* are akin to putting feet to our faith. They are calls to action in living others-focused lives that come out of who we are in Christ, as emphasized in God's Word.

The following are the seven Be-Attitudes and Liberties. These are listed in a natural cadence and flow with the intention of each being practiced every day. However, they are not a legalistic set of rules that each demand to be followed and checked off the list. Life is a journey of unpredictability, and certainly, when you follow Jesus it will be filled with unpredictability and adventure! It could very well be that one day you practice two of the seven, or perhaps all seven but not in exact order. That is okay. The goal is to cultivate continual mindfulness for them all and to develop the good habit of using them to draw closer to God.

The *Be*-Attitudes:

Be-Attitude	Liberties
*Bre*athe	Live—to the fullest
Be Still	Let Go—of worries; Listen—to God
*Be*loved	Love—God and others
*Be*am	Light—receive from God, shine to others
*Be*lieve	Learn—to live by faith through His Word
Be Joyful	Laugh—cultivating praise, thanks, and prayer
*Be*hold	Look—for divine moments, God at work

Continually drawing close to God is the point of all this (not a checklist of tasks to adhere to), and the Be-Attitudes, when practiced, will provide the means for drawing and staying close to our Lord.

Also, there isn't a specific timeframe, or clock, in which to practice. You can spend fifteen minutes on all seven, fifty minutes, an hour, or more. Let the Holy Spirit guide you in the practice and then time will take care of itself.

For the rest of our time together, we'll dive deeper into the meaning of each Be-Attitude, explore the scriptural context around them, and develop some practical behaviors that can be applied in our devotional time with the Lord. Let's go!

CHAPTER 3

*B*reathe

||||||||||||||||||||||||||

*"The Spirit of God has made me, and the
breath of the Almighty gives me life."*
~ Job 33:4, NKJV

Each one of us has a wonderful companion who is with us from
the moment we're born until the moment we die. This companion is unequivocally invested in us—our well-being and
literally our very life—and is a friend who will never leave us,
no matter what. This friend is completely selfless and unceasingly
attentive. Everything he does is for our vitality. Yet we often treat
this lifelong companion with contempt, or at the very least, indifference. We often act as if he doesn't exist, and yet, without him,
we would cease to exist. Who is this devoted, loyal companion we
like and need to have around, but often take for granted? "He" is
oxygen—the very air we breathe.

> *"There are these two young fish swimming along and they happen to meet an older fish swimming the other way, who nods at them and says 'Morning boys. How's the water?' And the two young fish swim on for a bit, and then eventually one of them looks at the other and goes, 'What is water?'"*
> *~ David Foster Wallace's 2005 commencement speech to the graduating class at Kenyon College*

What is oxygen? For us, it's what water is to fish. It's all around us, in us, and sustains us, yet we hardly give it a thought. And breathing it is so vital, but it just might be on our top five list of things we never acknowledge. After all, it's a birthright, an entitlement (so we think), but do we really own our breath? Can we prevent it from being taken away? We can use it, and we can control it to some extent, but we can't create it. If we cannot manufacture it naturally, on our own, then who does? Who supplies it? Who maintains it? Whoever that is, shouldn't we hold that person in the highest regard? Whoever has the power to give and to take away (especially our breath!)—that's the one who deserves all our attention and respect; all our reverence and our loyalty, this King of O_2. Believers know who this person is. It's God. He said, "I will put breath in you, and you will come to life. Then you will know that I am the LORD" (Ezekiel 37:6, NIV). As Job proclaimed, "Naked I came from my Mother's womb, and naked I shall return there. The LORD gave, and the LORD has taken away; blessed be the name of the LORD" (Job 1:21, NKJV). Only God wields this power over life and death.

Many Eastern meditation practices incorporate breathing as a vital part of meditation, and we have learned so much about how to work with our breath from their techniques, but often their emphasis is on "your" breath, as if you and I own it. We can use it, and we can also learn to control the breath we're given, but we don't own it. Our life, then, is literally in God's hands: "God created the heavens and stretched them out; He fashioned the earth and all that lives there; He gave life and breath to all its people" (Isaiah 42:5, GNBDC).

We wake up every day to a newly wrapped present sitting on our nightstand, with every sunrise, a new gift for us to open. This gift from God is the breath of life. Let us give praise to Him for this immeasurable gift! If we receive nothing else, we can always praise Him for continuing to fill our lungs with oxygen, for another day of life! As the Nicene Creed declares, "I believe in the Holy Spirit, the Lord, *the Giver of life* . . . "

In the Be-Attitude of *Breathe*, we set out every morning to deliberately attend to our breath, and as we do, we are acknowledging God's lordship over our lives and joining the psalmist in singing, "Let everything that has breath praise the LORD" (Psalm 150:6, NIV).

This is where the spiritual realm comes in. I find two insights in this passage. One, we praise God—the Creator of life and breath—because we have the gift of breath, because we're alive. The nonbeliever uses breath in meditation to enliven the physical body and to light up what they refer to as their energy field. The believer uses breath in meditation to praise God. It's an act of worship. It's acknowledging that "He who has the Son has [eternal] life" (1 John 5:12, NKJV).

My second observation is that, if our breath is all we have, then we should consider ourselves rich beyond measure and extremely blessed, since our breath is the ultimate need, knowing that nothing is more valuable and essential; without it, we would cease to exist. It's a reminder that the simple things are what matter the most. The simple things are often the most profound. It's a reminder that life is a gift.

Gratitude for the simple yet profound gift of breath—the gift of life—is accentuated in a scene from the movie *The Titanic*, in which Leonardo DiCaprio's free-spirited character Jack Dawson responds to a stinging question about his nomadic life from Rose's arrogant and condescending mother, as she quips while taking a sip of champagne from her crystal goblet,

"And you find that sort of rootless existence appealing, do you?"

To which Jack responds, "Well, yes, ma'am, I do . . . I mean, I got everything I need right here with me. I got air in my lungs and a few blank sheets of paper. I mean, I love waking up in the morning not knowing what's gonna happen or, who I'm gonna meet, where I'm gonna wind up. Just the other night I was sleeping under a bridge and now here I am on the grandest ship in the world having champagne with you fine people. I figure life's a gift and I don't intend on wasting it. You don't know what hand you're gonna get dealt next. You learn to take life as it comes at you . . . to make each day count."[3]

Jack's response resonates with us. His free spirit is born out of wonder, genuine appreciation, and the type of simplicity we long to get back to. The simplest things are the most profound. "I've got air in my lungs . . . ". He lives spontaneously, knowing that each day is not an entitlement but a gift. His awareness of

3   "Jack Dawson Quotes - Titanic." FicQuotes. Copyright 2022 — FicQuotes.Com. Accessed February 5, 2022. https://ficquotes.com/jack-dawson-titanic-1997-character-quotes/.

this enables each day to matter, to be valued, not wasted. He has embraced life.

We find Jack at ease and comfortable in his own skin, whereas we find Rose, played by Kate Winslet, conveying the opposite demeanor—exasperated and anxious. We can tend to be more like Rose than Jack. Like her, we may be facing a situation where we're caught in the trappings of life, even when those things might be providing comfort and security, and as a result, we're feeling stifled, controlled, formed into someone else's mold, smothered by the things of this world. In another scene, the one in which Jack's and Rose's worlds first collide, we find Rose literally running away from her circumstances, escaping in a rush from the front of the ship to the back. By the time she passes Jack at the stern, she is out of breath and ready to end it all. There, we find Jack relaxed on a bench gazing at the stars.

Some days we're Jack. Some days we're Rose. And when exasperated and out of breath like her, let that be a sign that something is off and needs to change. My wife knows I'm having a Rose-like moment when she hears from me what she calls "the sigh." It's a sign to her that my anxiety is spiking. It's then when I need to tell myself (or be told!) to relax . . . take a deep breath . . . regroup . . . settle down. I've heard Jill say to me many times, "Calm down, Captain. Take a breath." If we would just pay attention, the cadence of our breathing would tell us a lot about our state of mind and emotion.

The Practice and Benefits of Proper Breathing

There are countless articles online regarding how to properly breathe to maintain good health. If you Google "breathing exercise," it'll produce over 185,000,000 results! Knowing how to manage the small act of breathing effectively can help us relax, reduce stress, improve sleep, strengthen exercise, aid in digestion, and more. The benefits to our physiology are endless and a big reason for the surge in popularity of mindfulness training and yoga. Some articles even state that many of the ailments we suffer from today are due to improper and inefficient breathing. As a runner, I know all too well what happens when my breathing is off. If I'm inhaling and exhaling too rapidly, I hyperventilate and inevitably my physical body shuts down and forces me to stop and "catch my breath"—which is to say, I need more oxygen! Conversely, when the cadence of my breath is even and I'm moving my body in rhythm to it, I will hit the heralded state of flow that all runners strive for. Oxygen, the catalyst for flow, is working through my body like a well-oiled car. Proper breathing matters!

Learning how to breathe right does wonders for the heart. Studies show that passion and anxiety have the same heart rate. Both register at approximately 120 beats per minute, yet one is beneficial and one can wreak havoc! The difference between the two is in how the heart beats at that pace: The passionate heart beats rhythmically, the anxious heart, erratically. An erratic heartbeat, especially when prolonged, means danger, as it inflicts heavy strain on the heart muscles. When we learn how to control our breath, we're able to command our physiology to a place of smooth cadence and ultimate health.

Who Maintains This Delicate Balance?

It may seem like oxygen is a ubiquitous resource, but when we consider the vast expanse of the universe, then how mankind can trek up to the point where the amount of oxygen is dangerously low (think Mt. Everest), we realize how unique O_2 is within the canopy of our world. Miraculously, it continues to be contained within Earth's boundaries, and despite the myriad of changes over the millennia in our ecology, somehow the level of oxygen has remained consistently at the critical 20.95 percent makeup within the atmosphere. If that level were to change by slight degrees in either direction, we'd either asphyxiate to death having too little, or we'd burn to death having too much. How is this delicate balance held together?

Mankind has always been very good at finding new ways to challenge the ecosystem. Despite this, the balance of what's required in our atmosphere to live has been maintained. We cannot claim responsibility for this extraordinary maintenance, no more than we can claim responsibility for enabling the sun to rise and set. As believers, we know that everything created has a Creator and that Creator is God. Oxygen is His invention, and He used it to build the universe and to breathe life into us. By God's design, approximately two thirds of the human body is oxygen, making it the most abundant element in the body. Oxygen is also the most abundant element in the earth's crust (about 47 percent by mass) and the third most common element in the universe—as stars burn hydrogen and helium, oxygen becomes more abundant. O_2 is unstable in our planet's atmosphere and must be constantly replenished by photosynthesis in green plants. Without life, our atmosphere would contain almost no O_2. If we discover any other planets with atmospheres rich in oxygen, we will know that life is almost certainly present on these planets; significant quantities of O_2 will only exist on planets when it is released by living things.[4] "By the word of the LORD the heavens were made, and all the host of them by the breath of His mouth" (Psalm 33:6, NKJV). God spoke life into being—the heavens, the stars, you, and me.

---

4   Stewart, Dr. Doug. "Facts about Oxygen." Chemicool. Copyright © 2022 chemicool.com. Accessed February 5, 2022. https://www.chemicool.com/elements/oxygen–facts.html.

Oxygen—the breath of God—is abundant in the body, the earth, the universe, and the stars. Oxygen is the foundational element of God's creation; where we find oxygen, we find life.

"And the LORD God formed man of the dust of the ground and breathed into his nostrils the breath of life; and man became a living being" (Genesis 2:7, NKJV). The breath of God gives us life. He is the source of life and He used His breath to create it in us. He's the One who deserves all our attention, all our loyalty. He has gifted us with the very essence of what establishes and keeps us alive.

||||||||||||||||||||||||||||||||||||||||||||||||||||||||||||||||||||||||||||||||||||||||||||||||||||||||

The original Hebrew word used in Genesis 2:7 for "breath" is *neshamah*, which means both "breath" and "spirit." God gave us both as He awakened our existence into the world.

||||||||||||||||||||||||||||||||||||||||||||||||||||||||||||||||||||||||||||||||||||||||||||||||||||||||

The Greek word for breath is *psuche* (psoo-khay) which is the root of the English words "psyche" and "psychology"—a person's distinct identity and unique personality.

||||||||||||||||||||||||||||||||||||||||||||||||||||||||||||||||||||||||||||||||||||||||||||||||||||||||

In the book of Job, Job's friend Elihu makes the following statement: "The Spirit of God has made me, and the breath of the Almighty gives me life" (Job 33:4, NKJV). Elihu was surely thinking of the words in Genesis 2:7 when he said this. We are made by God, created by His breath, and it's His breath that gives us life. Breath is Spirit is Life: "But when you give them breath, they are created; you give new life to the earth" (Psalm 104:30, GNBDC).

When Jesus appeared to His disciples after being raised from the dead, He said to them, "'Peace be with you. As the Father sent me, so I send you.' *Then He breathed on them* and said, 'Receive the Holy Spirit'" (John 20:21–22, GNBDC, emphasis mine).

The Greek word used in John 20:22 for "breathed" is the only instance of it in the New Testament, but it's the very one used by the Greek translators of the Hebrew Bible in the verse we read earlier—Genesis 2:7—when God breathed into man's nostrils and gave Him life.[5] Christ was, quite literally, breathing new life into man to make him a new creation by the power of the Holy Spirit. Breath is life. It's the very Spirit that sustains us. And in His breath is peace, not turmoil. He calms the wind. When we receive His breath of peace, no storm or titanic situation will overtake us.

In many secular practices, there is no acknowledgment of the source of breath apart from self. How absurd! Or they credit the "universe" as the source. Question: how does the "universe" suddenly stop (or start) sending oxygen your way? Isn't that paramount to having made a decision, and aren't decisions made by people rather than ambiguous entities like "the universe"? Christian meditation and breathing exercise, however, begins with the acknowledgment that we are merely recipients of the breath a divine authority—God—provides us. The sobering fact is that knowing God gives and God takes away (as we learned from Job 1:21), we understand that He alone decides whether we'll take the next breath. We can't demand it. Like salvation, it is simply and purely a gift. God is the source of it all.

"Who has ascended into heaven and descended?
Who has gathered the wind in His fists?
Who has bound the waters in His garment?

---

5   Pink, Arthur W. Essay. *Exposition of the Gospel of John.* Grand Rapids, MI: Zondervan, 1982, p. 1100.

> Who has established all the ends of the earth?
> What is His name, and what is His Son's name?
> Certainly you know!"
> ~ Proverbs 30:5, AMP

The wind doesn't obey us; it obeys Christ. The air we breathe is not subservient to human hands or minds. We see this in the following passage: "Then He arose and rebuked the wind, and said to the sea, 'Peace, be still!' And the wind ceased and there was a great calm" (Mark 4:39, NKJV).

||||||||||||||||||||||||||||||||||||||||||||||||||||||||||||||||||||||||||||||||||||||||||||||||||||||||

The Greek word for wind in Mark 4:39 is *aer*, which is air and it comes from the root word *aemi*, "to breath unconsciously."
Only He can still the air. Only He can control the breath.

||||||||||||||||||||||||||||||||||||||||||||||||||||||||||||||||||||||||||||||||||||||||||||||||||||||||

There was a leader of the synagogue named Jairus whose daughter had just died. Upon being told this, Jesus entered his house and went back to the bedroom where she lay. Jesus took her hand and said to her in a loud voice, "My child, get up!" Scripture states that "at that moment her life returned, and she immediately stood up!" (Luke 8:55, NKJV). Other translations state that her spirit returned. Spirit is life and life is breath. The spirit, or *pnuema*, is breath. Only Jesus Christ has the power to make it return.

Another example is Stephen. As Stephen was being battered to death with stones, he cried out saying, "Lord Jesus, receive my spirit!" (Acts 7:59) And, as Jesus "breathed His last," He cried out in a loud voice, "Father, into your hands I commit My Spirit" (Luke 23:46, NKJV).

The word "breathed" in the Luke passage, and "Spirit" in both passages, comes from the same root word *pneo*, which means "to breathe, to blow." The Spirit and the breath go together. The breath of God gives us life when we are first born and the Spirit of God—The Holy Spirit—gives us life when we are reborn as we profess our faith in Jesus Christ and are welcomed into the kingdom of God.

In *Plan Be*, the very first thing we do upon waking is to praise the Lord for the breath He gives us. And in every breath, we worship Him. The breath He gives us alone is cause for worship! Essentially, we are praising Him for another day alive, for having air in our lungs and for the capacity to use it, as we attend to our breathing and as we begin our quiet time with Him. Let everything that has breath praise the Lord!

Practical *Behaviors* for Learning How to *Breathe*:

Immediately after waking, let's practice what I call the "Big Three"—three rounds of three deep inhales and exhales, varied through our nose and mouth. The purpose of this breathing exercise is to pump fresh oxygen into our bodies and awaken our autonomic nervous systems. The autonomic nervous system controls the aspects of our body that aren't consciously directed—our breathing, our heartbeat, and our digestive system. This exercise is like a wake-up call for our system and will be a refreshing start to our day!

The Big Three is simple and only takes one or two minutes from start to finish. We can perform this breathing exercise sitting or standing, our body open-postured (not scrunched), relaxed but in a way that we'll be able to expand our lungs and core.

"Big Three" Breathing Practice:

Each inhale and exhale is deep, with enough force to hear our breath. Allow the belly to expand on inhale and contract/relax on exhale.

Round 1: Inhale through the nose deeply, then exhale through the nose deeply. Do this three times.

Round 2: Inhale through the nose deeply, then exhale through the mouth deeply. Do this three times.

Round 3: Inhale through the mouth deeply, then exhale through the mouth deeply. Do this three times.

I find during this time that I tend to yawn, which is perfectly okay. Yawning is a good thing—it's simply our body's way of bringing more oxygen into the bloodstream and expelling excess carbon dioxide.

The Big Three is an exercise that will wake us up and get our motors running. The lungs will wake up, the heart will wake up, the blood will oxygenate, and the mind will become more alert. Whenever I perform this exercise, I visualize feeding my brain with the oxygen I'm bringing into my body. The more we practice, the better we'll become at deepening the inhale and exhale. The deeper we breathe, the more relaxed we'll become.

The next technique is more meditative and is designed to transition into a nice rhythm and flow in our morning. This is where we really connect with God as we gently enter into our quiet time with Him. It will also be the transition into the next Be-Attitude: *Be* Still.

"Smooth Seven" Breathing Practice:

The "Smooth Seven" breathing practice is calmer and more rhythmic than the Big Three. It's called "Smooth Seven" because we'll take longer and less forceful breaths in through our nose for a count of seven seconds, then exhale through our mouth for another count of seven seconds.

Inhale for seven seconds. Exhale for seven seconds. Then repeat this seven times.

The force is more of a normal breath, quiet enough that if someone were sitting next to us, they wouldn't hear our breathing.

As we breathe in, we'll make them belly breaths, allowing our belly to expand on the inhale and contract on the exhale. The point is to feel the smooth flow and develop a rhythm in our breathing that is not forced, but natural. We can reduce or increase the number of rounds (seven is a guideline). The goal is to feel a sense of peace and calm. Our body will tell us if more is needed.

The Smooth Seven practice sets our breathing cadence for the day. The more we practice this upon awakening, the more we'll naturally go back to it during the day. It's also an excellent way to re-center whenever we're faced with a stressful situation or simply need to refocus.

Remember how anxiety's heart rate is erratic while passion's heart rate is consistent and even? The Smooth Seven will help us master the state of flow in our breathing and develop the proper pattern that results in an alert yet calm, consistent, and even state of mind.

"Prair" (Prayer + Air)

At first, it'll be necessary to count our breaths as we practice until the cadence is developed and we become familiar with the timing. After we gain more experience, it'll be possible to replace counting with prayer. I've found that with the following counting technique, I don't have to look at my watch. Rather than counting, "One, two, three . . ." and so on, I count, "One one, two two, three three . . ." Counting in this fashion more accurately keeps the actual time. As a play on words, I remind myself to pray during this time, visualizing the word "prair" (prayer and air).

Instead of counting, we can replace it with a short scripture or a prayer of our own. An example of a prair is "Lord, Your will, not mine, be done," which we repeat on every inhale and exhale. This will help us to focus on God as we prepare to fellowship with Him in the next Be-Attitude (plus it's a lot more meaningful and fun than simply counting our breath!).

As an alternate to reciting a "prair," we can opt to fill our minds with positive thoughts as we inhale, then release any negative thoughts as we exhale. For example, as we inhale, we breathe in joy, and as we exhale, we breathe out sadness. It's a very spiritual, life-giving exercise to inhale the positive and then expel the negative, to replace any stress, worry, fear, or anxiety with light, joy, and hope.

Other Breathing Practices

We can practice any of the breathing exercises at any time during the day, not just in our morning quiet time. I've gone to these exercises often as a means for re-centering my spirit and alleviating stress, as well as the following:

Box Breathing:

I learned this from Mark Divine, U.S. Navy SEALs Commander (Retired) and author of *The Way of the SEAL: Think Like an Elite Warrior to Lead and Succeed.*

Inhale for four seconds. Hold for four seconds. Exhale four seconds. Hold four seconds. Repeat four times (seconds and repeats can vary).

The Wim Hof Method:

Wim Hof is widely known as "The Iceman," due to his cold therapy method as a way to become healthier. Wim Hof has also developed a popular breathing technique that can produce physiological benefits. You can learn all about it at www.wimhofmethod. com and can also download his app by simply searching for "Wim Hof Method" in your phone or device's app store.

His breathing practice involves short, powerful bursts of inhaling and exhaling, up to 30–40 times, and also includes stages of holding breath. I recommend Wim's method after having spent time with more basic breathing practices. Remember, be sure to add "prair" to these additional techniques.

Once we begin our day with proper, attentive breathing, we'll set ourselves up for a very tuned-in and intentional quiet time with the Lord, one in which we're completely present and ready to be filled with His presence. When we are fully awake and the oxygen is flowing through our body, we'll be prepared to focus on fellowship with our Lord with intentionality and wholehearted connection. We will be equipped to draw closer to Him in silence and stillness as we lean into the next Be-Attitude, ***Be Still***.

|||||||||||||||||||||||||||||||||||||||||||||||||||||||||||||||||||||||||||||||||||||||||

YOUR *BE*ACON: Breathe Basics (2 minutes)
- Find a comfortable, quiet place to sit.
- Invite Jesus into your heart.
- Take a deep breath in (allow your stomach to expand).
- Let a deep breath out (stomach contracts).
- Repeat three times.
- If you have time, continue but in a slower, smoother fashion for two more minutes.

|||||||||||||||||||||||||||||||||||||||||||||||||||||||||||||||||||||||||||||||||||||||||

*BE*NEDICTION

"Now the God of peace, who brought up from the dead the great Shepherd of the sheep through the blood of the eternal covenant, even Jesus our Lord, equip you in every good thing to do His will, working in us that which is pleasing in His sight, through Jesus Christ, to whom be the glory forever and ever. Amen." (Hebrews 13:20–21, NASB)

How has this Be-Attitude encouraged you?

_____

_____

_____

_____

_____

What are some positive action steps that you can take after learning this practice?

_____

_____

_____

_____

_____

What are some "prairs" that you can use?

_____

_____

_____

_____

Make a list of positive words to inhale and negative words to exhale during your breathing practice:

_____

_____

_____

_____

_____

CHAPTER 4

Be Still

||||||||||||||||||||||||

"Be still and know that I am God;
I will be exalted among the nations,
I will be exalted in the earth!"
~ Psalm 46:10, NKJV

n *Plan Be*, we practice stillness before God so we might fellowship with Him, honor Him, and cultivate a desire to want what He wants. God longs to have a deep personal relationship with us.

||||||||||||||||||||||||||||||||||||||||||||||||||||||||||||||||||||||||||||||||||||||||||||||||||||||||

The Hebrew word for "be still" is *raphah*, which
means to be quiet and to let go.

||||||||||||||||||||||||||||||||||||||||||||||||||||||||||||||||||||||||||||||||||||||||||||||||||||||||

As we spend quality time with Him, putting Him first in our day, we will grow in our intimacy together. Quietness before Him stills the soul. Listening fills our hearts and minds with Him. He longs to guide us, instruct us, and teach us in the way we should go, for He is the Way, the Truth, and the Life. As we calm our hearts before Him, giving full attention to Him, He will be honored, and God takes pleasure in those who honor Him. He will fill our hearts with His love:

> *"The LORD is good to those who wait for*
> *him, to the soul who seeks him.*
> *It is good that one should wait quietly for*
> *the salvation of the LORD." (Lamentations*
> *3:25–26, ESV)*

Lay It All Down

In the Be-Attitude of *Be* Still, we acknowledge who has control: God. We surrender to His lordship. The disciples learned this in dramatic fashion, right after they felt they were going to die in a storm—an overwhelming squall that was having great success in swamping their boat. They were working frantically with all their strength to prevent death by drowning. Where was Jesus? He was in the back of the boat sleeping. The storm didn't concern Him, for He holds power over the storms.

"And they awoke Him and said to him, 'Teacher, do you not care that we are perishing?'" (Mark 4:38, NKJV). So the Teacher did this: "He awoke and rebuked the wind and said to the sea, 'Peace! Be still!' And the wind ceased, and there was a great calm. He said to them, 'Why are you so afraid? Have you still no faith?' And they were filled with great fear and said to one another,

'Who then is this, that even the wind and the sea obey him?'" (Mark 4:39—41, ESV).

Their Teacher had suddenly become their Lord. He certainly is our Teacher, though as the disciples dramatically realized , He is so much more. He is Creator and Lord, Master of the elements and better yet, Master over our lives. I don't believe the primary take-away in this story is to learn how to stay calm during storms, or even that Jesus will always silence them and restore calm, especially on our timeline. These things may indeed happen on occasion, but I believe the main takeaway is that when the inevitable storms do come, He is there, He will remain, and He will see us through. His promise made in the Old Testament remains today— "For the LORD your God goes with you; He will never leave you nor forsake you" (Deuteronomy 31:6, NIV). We must have faith.

As we come to Christ every morning, quietly sitting in His presence—a presence that we know is always there, no matter the calm or chaos—we learn by the grace and leading of the Holy Spirit to relax. In the stillness, in the silent moments, the Spirit cultivates in us an ability to wait on Him, and there is wisdom in the waiting, for waiting builds strength of character: "Wait patiently for the LORD; be strong and courageous. Wait patiently for the LORD!" (Psalm 27:14, BSB)

It may often seem like nothing is happening, but in solitude, God is planting wisdom in our hearts, and through the continual experience of being still we come to understand how active God is and learn to not mistake His silence for complacency. He is always at work. Scripture says that "God is working in you, giving you the desire and the power to do what pleases Him" (Philippians 2:13, NLT). This passage doesn't say that God does the work on our behalf while we sit idly by. It does say that in our connection with Him, He empowers our spirits with all that He is, so that we, being in His likeness in every way, can then *do according to His will*. Time alone with Him, in quiet connection and prayer, will infuse us with His character, empowering us with His desires and His power. Therefore, it's vital to prioritize personal time with Him. In this time He will transform us, renewing our minds and building our character, especially in the seeking and the waiting, in the sitting and the silence.

"Letting go" is an important part of our quiet time before the Lord. It may be the main part. It's hard to remain quiet in our spirits when there's an internal storm brewing. Often, we wake up immediately confronted by the concerns of the day, or worse yet, are woken up at night by those concerns. Let's resolve to set these at the feet of our Savior. He—both Teacher and Commander of creation—is in our boat; let's call out to Him. He will arise and see us through to the other side.

Hebrews 12:1–2 (NKJV) illustrates how letting go of (or "laying aside") what we were not meant to carry is crucial to running our lifelong race well:

> *"Therefore we also, since we are surrounded by so great a cloud of witnesses, let us lay aside every weight, and the sin which so easily ensnares us, and let us run with endurance the race that is set before us, looking unto Jesus, the author and finisher of our faith, who for the joy that was set before Him endured the cross, despising the shame, and has sat down at the right hand of the throne of God."*

We lay aside all the junk that immediately fills our minds upon waking. The only way we can truly do this is to have someone capable and willing to take and deal with the junk. God has this! We don't have to worry! We relax and rest in Him, the One who has finished this race and will be with us continually to guide us through our earthly finish line into eternity. While on Earth, endurance is needed to run well and run long, and we will not be able to run effectively while carrying weights and burdens.

C. S. Lewis once wrote, "God doesn't want something from us. He simply wants us." Let's come to Him embracing the freedom He offers to simply fellowship with Him. He isn't looking for us to deliver on anything, although He is always ready to take our burdens. Now that is kindness, mercy, and love!

In his book *Delighting in God*, A.W. Tozer wrote, "God's greatest delight is to bring [us] into His Presence." It gives God joy to have us in His company! We shouldn't shy away from Him for any reason since there isn't a reason why He wouldn't welcome us with open arms. His Son settled any reason at the cross, and now we have full access to Him!

A Let

In the sport of tennis, there are three potential outcomes when serving the ball to an opponent: a successful serve to the opponent's service box, an unsuccessful serve that doesn't hit inside their service box called a "fault," or something of a do-over called a "let." A let is when the serve first hits the top of the net, then drops into the opponent's service box. This type of serve is not counted against the server. It's always a relief when serving a let because it negates a fault, and the server is given another chance as if that serve never happened.

As I read in God's Word to *let* go, it reminds me of a do-over, of a chance to begin again and to allow ourselves grace at that moment, knowing God doesn't consider us at fault. There is no limit to the number of lets allowed in tennis. Likewise, God never sets a limit on the number of lets we're given as we learn how to serve in this game of life: "Because of the LORD's great love we are not consumed, for His compassions never fail. They are new every morning; great is your faithfulness" (Lamentations 3:22–23, NIV). We should never fault ourselves to the point where we feel we cannot come to Jesus. Oftentimes we handle our guilt and shame and the sense of failure, of any sin, as a disqualifier that prevents us from even stepping onto the court.

However, wonderful things happen when we let go. At Jesus' command, the fishermen let go of their nets and the result was 153 fish (see John 21). Let us, too, start by letting go.

No one in my life embodies this Be–Attitude better than my wife, Jill. There is a sense of profound peace in her life, a stillness in her soul that is infinitely attractive, and I've witnessed countless times where people have been drawn to her because of her calming presence. She teaches preschool and her children (and parents) adore her because she radiates an approachable, contagious calm. What most don't know is how Jill has conquered so much adversity in her life, and this has happened by her drawing close to God and trusting Him to love and protect her when others weren't capable or willing. He showed her how to let go of problems and cares so that her heart could be open to Him continually. And in this process, God has poured into her heart a beautiful spirit of giving, and what I've learned from her is how to receive the unending grace that Christ freely offers. She is truly a free person.

Sit in the Stillness

The call to be still in Psalm 46 is in response to the writer's experience of fear, trouble, the rage of nations, calamity on the earth (roaring waters, shaking mountains), and war. Sounds contemporary, doesn't it? The remedy in Psalm 46 is God. He "is our refuge and strength, a very present help in trouble" (verse 1). God is in the midst of all the chaos and yet "will not be moved" (verse 6). We can let go of the fear and we can sit calm before Him because "the LORD of hosts is with us" (verse 7). When we're tempted to fear the chariots, he burns them. When we fear the bow, He breaks it. When we fear the spear, He cuts it in two. The psalm ends with this: "The LORD of hosts *is* with us; The God of Jacob *is* our refuge. SELAH" (Psalm 46:11, NKJV, emphasis mine). So, we can let go of the fear, the anxiety, the sadness, doubt, and worry. God is with us. He cannot be defeated by our enemies. Let's take refuge in Him.

Exodus 14:14 (NIV) says, "The LORD will fight for you; you need only to be still." The Egyptians were in hot pursuit of the Israelites, and the Israelites "feared greatly" (verse 10). They thought they'd die in the wilderness and argued that it would've been better to have remained slaves in Egypt. Fear does that. It compels us to retreat to the familiar, the way it used to be, even when it means returning to what we despised and originally tried to get out of.

It can be very difficult to comprehend that the Lord will act on our behalf, especially amid overwhelming odds. But when we find ourselves at the end of our rope, this is precisely when God will show up. He will come through! We have to press into Him to possess the courage to carry on. Pressing into Him takes work on our part—seeking Him out and trusting in Him.

For, as the Scripture says, "Just a little while longer, and He who is coming will come; He will not delay. My righteous people, however, will believe and live; but if any of them turns back, I will not be pleased with them" (Hebrews 10:37–38, GNT).

When we're still before God, when we let go of the things that we can't handle—giving them over to the One who can—and when we listen to Him and are comforted and equipped by Him, He will encourage our hearts, build our faith, and give us strength to move forward. And the result will be our declaration as believers: "We are not people who turn back and are lost. Instead, we have faith and are saved" (Hebrews 10:39, GNT).

The key is in coming to God every single day—multiple times a day. David wrote, "Morning, noon, and night I cry out in my distress, and the LORD hears my voice" (Psalm 55:17, NLT). The morning is just a fantastic way to start! David, amid pursuit by his enemies, by the "crushing pressure of their opposition," with his heart in anguish by the betrayal of a friend, decided to let go and let God.

God knows us through and through. As we read throughout Psalm 139, our God knows, understands, and comprehends us. He saw us before we were ever conceived: "Your eyes saw my substance, being yet unformed" (verse 16). Because of all this, David exclaims, "How precious [esteemed, prized, valued] also are your thoughts to me, O God! How great is the sum of them! If I should count then, they would be more in number than the sand; when I awake, I am still with you" (Psalm 139:17–18, NKJV).

David, having realized the all-seeing, all-knowing character of God, humbled himself under His lordship. As far as knowing how to live, David surrendered a "let me tell *You* . . . " mentality, instead praying to God with the humble stance of, "Lord, please tell *me*, search *me*, lead *me*." May we strive toward this level of submission and come to the Lord with the same humility. Because of

God's unending thoughts toward him, toward every one of us, we can proclaim, like David did, "When I awake, I am still with you."

Like David, the apostle Peter experienced what it meant to let go and let God, and he advised the Jewish believers who were persecuted and scattered abroad: "Humble yourselves, therefore, under the mighty hand of God so that at the proper time He may exalt you, casting all your anxieties on Him, because He cares for you" (1 Peter 5:6–7, ESV).

When we put God first and are still before Him, we honor Jesus' command: "Seek first the kingdom of God and His righteousness" (Matthew 6:33, NKJV). Jesus exhorted His followers to do this in response to and as a remedy for their worries, a topic He addressed no less than six times in this particular discourse found in the book of Matthew. His response to each worry was, essentially, *God's got this! He knows your needs!*

David practiced quietly waiting upon God, and God alone. He did not trust in man to build strongholds for him, to support his plans, to be his refuge in times of trouble: "My soul waits in silence for God alone; from Him comes my salvation. He alone is my rock and my salvation, my stronghold; I will not be greatly shaken" (Psalm 62:1–2, NASB). He repeats this a little further down in verse 5: "My soul, wait in silence for God alone. For my hope is from Him." It's as if David is coaching himself, reminding his soul to place trust and hope in God alone. Let us remind ourselves as well!

Throughout this wonderful Psalm, David instructs himself on waiting upon, resting in, and trusting in the only One who can be trusted: his rock and his salvation, God. And he reaches out to us in this psalm with this encouragement as well. I can almost hear him emphatically exhorting us when he says, "Trust Him at all times, you people; pour out your hearts before Him; God is a refuge for us. Selah" (Psalm 62:8, NASB).

This stillness before Him cultivates a very important virtue, one that the apostle James said leads to wholeness (read James 1:4), and that virtue, or fruit, is patience.

"Be still in the presence of the LORD, and wait patiently for him to act. Don't worry about evil people who prosper or fret about their wicked schemes" (Psalm 37:7, NLT).

Active Rest

As we sit still before the Lord, He develops an "active rest" in our hearts that is seasoned with calm and patience. If we feel like we don't have time to meditate before Him, then we're precisely the ones who need it! As we meditate quietly before Him, we are choosing to peacefully and deliberately ease into our day. By placing God first and taking time to connect with Him, we reshape our lives into ones of tranquility, led by the only One who could truly guide us. We develop a smooth, unhurried rhythm to life, knowing that He goes before us and He's in control. Throughout time, He'll develop in our spirit a divine waiting, built on trust. Even when evil swirls around and threatens to capsize our boat, time with God and intimacy with Him will be like an anchor to stabilize us. As we read from David throughout Psalm 37, we will "fret not;" instead we'll trust in the Lord because we know He is our "fortress in times of trouble" (Psalm 27:39, NLT).

Plan Be is about being present, patient, and at peace. As we come before Him in stillness and solitude, we'll learn to cultivate an active rest—engaged in the act of letting go of the burdens we are not meant to carry—and calmly, with open hands, receive that which God intended for us to take all along.

Mother Teresa said it well: "We need to find God, and he cannot be found in noise and restlessness. God is the friend of silence. See how nature—trees, flowers, grass—grows in silence; see the stars, the moon, and the sun, how they move in silence . . . We need silence to be able to touch souls."

The following are practical ways to cultivate *Being* Still, to let go of negative forces which might otherwise attempt to rule our day, and to listen to our Master so that we can begin aright:

Practical *Be*haviors for Being Still:

- We should arise early, before anyone else. This will ensure the most peaceful and undistracted time for fellowship with God.
- Let our first words upon waking be to thank God for this new day He's given us.
- Know that God eagerly awaits our fellowship. He says this through the prophet Isaiah: "I will answer them before they even call to me. While they are still talking about their needs, I will go ahead and answer their prayers" (Isaiah 65:24, NLT). This is the kind of God we serve—one with an unending, unfathomable measure of love for each one of us and great anticipation for personal communion with us.
- As we prepare to be still before Him, let's treat each morning as a sacred time, one where we fulfill the command: "Seek first the kingdom of God and His righteousness, and all these things shall be added to you" (Matthew 6:33, NKJV).
- We should find a private, quiet, comfortable place to sit, a place where we'll not be interrupted.

- Sit physically still, relaxing the body (the *Bre*athe Be-Attitude will help here).

- Let's "Come boldly before His throne, that we may obtain mercy and find grace to help in time of need" (Hebrews 4:16, NKJV).

- Pray, "In the name of Jesus Christ my Lord and Savior, I come before your throne," inviting God into our hearts.

- We scan our minds and heart for any negative emotions (fears, anxieties, worry, sadness, anger, frustration) and let them go. Give them to God and then trust Him to deal with those emotions. Say "God, I let go of _____." Remember that when we practice breathing, a good way to start expelling negativity (literally) is when we're exhaling; we breathe in the positive and breathe out the negative. This quiet time of *Be*ing Still will help us deal further with any negativity that may be lingering from our time in the *Bre*athe Be-Attitude.

- Re-center, if the mind begins to fill up with chatter, by having a sacred word ready. The word may be "peace" or "love"; it doesn't matter, as long as it's one word and is positive.

- The sacred word is inspired by the daily audio meditation App, Encountering Peace, created by Drew Dickens. I encourage you to visit encounteringpeace.com for more information on his wonderful daily meditations.

- One tactic regarding thoughts coming in is to observe them as if they were clouds drifting by in the sky. If the thoughts are good and positive, we can say thanks to God for them. If the thoughts are negative, we give them over to God to handle and picture those clouds dissolving into thin air as He takes them. With negative thoughts we can pray, "Lord, I let go of _____," then simply release them to Him. If the chatter gets too great, we can say the sacred word to refocus.

- Cultivating stillness before God is not about emptying our minds. It's about ultimately filling them with positive things, as Paul encouraged others: "My friends, fill your minds with those things that are good and that deserve praise: things that are true, noble, right, pure, lovely, and honorable. Put into practice what you learned and received from me, both from my words and from my actions. And the God who gives us peace will be with you" (Philippians 4:8–9, GNT).

- When we spend time with God, He will fill our minds with good things! The Holy Spirit will help us to replace the negative with the positive, and we'll receive His peace.

- After letting go, we'll simply listen, cease any internal dialogue, sit in silence before Him, and simply take Him in. If we need to re-center again after being distracted, we can restate the sacred word, or say, "Lord, I'm listening."

- Soak in the fact that there's never a time when God doesn't want to be with us! He longs for our fellowship! He wants to love, guide, instruct, and teach us. Simply basking in His presence is the most important aspect of our day.

- Often in the Bible when we read about the word "wait," it includes a supplying of strength, healing, hope, exaltation, teaching, and courage from God. The act of waiting on God can be hard but is always good. The waiting periods of our life are strengthening periods. He is not silent or inactive during this time. God has not left us to help someone else. He, omnipresent and omniscient, is actively working in the waiting of all who call on Him.

- Time in silence with Him is worship. We are not focusing on outcomes, but simply on abiding, presence, and honoring an invitation to share time and space together. We're not trying to conjure up any unique feelings or invoke goosebumps. God exemplifies His power in the silence itself.
- How do we know when God is speaking to us? When God speaks, He will never contradict His Word. This will be covered in more detail later in the Be-Attitude of *Be*lieve as we study Scripture.

In *Be* Still, our hearts begin to shift from self-focus to surrender, and it's in the surrendering—the letting go—that we grow in faith, for we will experience God's strength at work in our hearts: "For thus said the LORD God, the Holy One of Israel, 'In returning and rest you shall be saved; in quietness and in trust shall be your strength'" (Isaiah 30:15, ESV).

To a desire in line with God's will, He gives grace; and to a desire outside God's will, He grants mercy. As we continue to seek His will, God will align our hearts to His.

||||||||||||||||||||||||||||||||||||||||||||||||||||||||||||||||||||||||||||||||||||||

YOUR *BE*ACON: Be Still Basics (3+ minutes)
- As you sit quietly, pray, "I am here Lord. I am listening."
- Simply remain silent. Allow His Spirit to guide you.
- Re-center with a sacred word if needed (e.g., "peace").

||||||||||||||||||||||||||||||||||||||||||||||||||||||||||||||||||||||||||||||||||||||

||||||||||||||||||||||||||||||||||||||||||||||||||||||||||||||||||||||||||||||||||||||||||||||||||||||||

In His grace, He supplies us.

In His mercy, He protects us.

In His grace, He strengthens us.

In His mercy, He sustains us.

||||||||||||||||||||||||||||||||||||||||||||||||||||||||||||||||||||||||||||||||||||||||||||||||||||||||

Let's close this Be-Attitude with a portion of the prayers from St. Patrick's Breastplate. Christ is continually with us! May we feel His wonderful presence as we learn to *Be* Still before Him:

Christ with me, Christ before me, Christ behind me,

Christ in me, Christ beneath me, Christ above me,

Christ on my right, Christ on my left,

Christ when I lie down, Christ when I sit down, Christ when I arise,

Christ in the heart of every man who thinks of me,

Christ in the mouth of everyone who speaks of me,

Christ in every eye that sees me,

Christ in every ear who hears me.

Are you feeling loved yet? God loves you beyond measure! This is what our next Be-Attitude is all about—God calls us His **Beloved.** And we are to simply bask in Him and be loved by Him. As we are still before Him, He will infuse our souls with His Spirit, and His Spirit is love.

BENEDICTION

"Now to Him who is able to keep you from stumbling and to present you blame-less before the presence of His glory with great joy, to the only God, our Savior, through Jesus Christ our Lord, be glory,

> *majesty, dominion, and authority, before all time and now and forever. Amen."* (Jude 24–25, ESV)

How has this Be-Attitude encouraged you?

_____
_____
_____
_____
_____

What are some positive actions you can take after learning this practice?

_____
_____
_____
_____
_____

What are some "sacred words" that you can use to keep centered on God in your quiet time?

_____
_____
_____
_____

CHAPTER 5

*Be*loved

Part 1: God's Love for Us

||||||||||||||||||||||||||||

*"For I am certain that nothing can sepa-
rate us from His love: neither death nor
life, neither angels nor other heavenly rulers or powers, neither the present nor the
future, neither the world above nor the world
below—there is nothing in all creation that
will ever be able to separate us from the love
of God which is ours through Christ Jesus
our Lord."*
~ Romans 8:38–39, GNBDC

Intimacy, relationship, understanding, knowledge, positivity,
enlightenment, spiritual discernment, and joy. All these virtues
supplied by God culminate in the greatest of all things: love. By

definition, God is love. It's His identity, His DNA. And it's the DNA of everyone who has professed faith in Him as well. The greatest goal and the constant lesson in life is this: love. Love is the strongest Be-Attitude. We can love because He first loved us. Love courses through the other Be-Attitudes. It's the thread that holds the whole tapestry together. As we cultivate intimacy with Him, surrender and rest in Him, expose our hearts to Him, and approach our day with positive eyes wide open to see Him at work in and around us, we cannot help but shine His light on others . . . and His light is love. Love becomes the natural expression of all who belong to Him.

Amazingly, God calls us beloved. Amazing, because due to our sin we don't deserve it, but He loves us anyway. He loves us unconditionally and His love is not something that we have to earn: it's a gift. Romans 5:8 (NKJV) declares that "God demonstrates His own love toward us, in that while we were still sinners, Christ died for us." Jesus paid the ultimate sacrifice and gave up His life to save us while humanity was in its worst state. God did not wait for us to get our act together before the sacrifice was made. Yet to this day, many are still trying to do that very thing—to earn their way into right standing with Him, taking it upon themselves to shed their sins and remove their own guilt.

Friends, this is the heart of the gospel, the good news: that Jesus Christ, perfectly God and perfectly man (from God yet born of the virgin Mary), lived among us and carried all our burdens—past, present, and future—to the cross where He died a sinner's death on our behalf so that we might live completely free of wrath and eternal damnation, and instead be justified before a holy and righteous God, now worthy through Jesus' sacrificial death and resurrection, to live eternally with the Godhead—Father, Son, and

Holy Spirit. This good news, this salvation, is a gift. We cannot earn it. Christ has done all this for us:

> "But God, being rich in mercy, because of His great love with which He loved us, even when we were dead in our transgressions, made us alive together with Christ (by grace you have been saved), and raised us up with Him, and seated us with Him in the heavenly places in Christ Jesus so that in the ages to come He might show the surpassing riches of His grace in kindness toward us in Christ Jesus. **For by grace you have been saved through faith; and that not of yourselves, it is the gift of God; not as a result of works, so that no one may boast.** For we are His workmanship, created in Christ Jesus for good works, which God prepared beforehand so that we would walk in them." (Ephesians 2:4–10, NASB, emphasis mine)

Being still with God, during dedicated time with Him in quiet reflection, we'll naturally segue into the *Be*loved Be-Attitude. At this point, you may be asking, "Okay. What else?" There's nothing else! Simply take time to receive Him! God will reveal His love toward you. Open your heart to receive His love. Yes, you are worthy of His love! He longs to show you how much He loves you! We can cry out to Him like the psalmist in saying, "Show me how much you love me, LORD, and save me according to Your promise" (Psalm 119:41, GNBDC).

The Parental Love of God

If you have children, you already know the reality of always loving them no matter what and of your desire to constantly show them how much you love them. This is the unconditional love of God. No matter what you did wrong yesterday or even in the last minute, His love awaits you with open arms in full acceptance. Will there be times of discipline? Of course! Hebrews 12:6 (NLT) says that "God disciplines those He loves." He does so *out of His love* to mold our character, protect us, and help us mature as Christians. And in verse 11 of the same chapter we read, "For the moment all discipline seems painful rather than pleasant, but later it yields the peaceful fruit of righteousness to those who have been trained by it." The key is in our perspective. Do we see discipline as punishment, or do we see it as training? If we see it as training, then we'll be on the road to reaching God's ultimate purpose, and that is the peaceful fruit of righteousness.

As parents, we fully understand this concept. The opposite of love is not punishment; it's indifference. Which is worse, a parent who disciplines to shape their child's life, ultimately, in a positive way, or a parent who simply doesn't care and allows the undisciplined child to suffer their own consequences? God is not indifferent. He loves you and will bless you when it's time to bless you and He will discipline you when it's time to discipline you. In either case, He acts out of His deep love for you. In His deep love, He has gifted you with the Holy Spirit and He is strongly determined to ensure you continue to "walk by the Spirit and not gratify the desires of the flesh" (Galatians 5:16, NIV):

> *"Now suppose one of you fathers is asked*
> *by his son for a fish; he will not give him a*
> *snake instead of a fish, will he? Or if he is*

asked for an egg, he will not give him a scor-
pion, will he? If you then, being evil, know
how to give good gifts to your children, how
much more will your heavenly Father give
the Holy Spirit to those who ask Him?" (Luke
11:1–13, NASB)

This is how God loves you, as a good Father: "See how much the Father has loved us! His love is so great that we are called God's children—and so, in fact, we are" (1 John 3:1, GNBDC). He calls you His child! You belong in the family of God and He will always be your Father. Once you've professed your faith in Him, there is nothing that you could do (or not do!) to no longer be part of His family!

This fact holds a lot of meaning for me. Like many, I grew up in a household that experienced a quite precarious father situation. My biological father was filled with rage and took it out on very important people in my life. He succumbed to the bottle and spun out in so many ways that, eventually, he was sent away. A few years later, my mom remarried to a delightful and loving man, but the later years proved to be rough and he gave in to the pressures of the world and left the home during my early teens (arguably one of the most pivotal times in a young man's life), so I was again without what should have been the continual presence of a dad.

They say that we tend to view God as a reflection of our earthly fathers. For me, that held true. Through my lenses, God did exist but stood aloof, pseudo-present, more in the periphery and watching from the shadows, ready to disengage if He found a better offer. In essence, like my real fathers, God to me was another authority figure that didn't love me enough to stay. As a young teen, I grew increasingly angry at God for becoming more distant and uninvolved. I viewed Him like the dad who never came to my baseball games. He lacked any interest in being part of my life. He simply didn't care.

Rush

To fill the void in my heart, I did what many preteens do who are stumbling around trying to find meaning and their place in the world. I wanted to forge an identity, so I escaped to music. I embraced progressive rock with all of its sophisticated instrumentation, notes, and time signatures. I took up drumming for the sheer challenge of becoming a musician (and perhaps more importantly, a legitimate way of pounding out my frustrations), and I immediately connected with the most intricately gifted artists that I could find, which came in the form of a super-talented Canadian rock trio named Rush. With arguably the world's best rock drummer in Neil Peart, what aspiring percussionist would not be drawn to this guy and this group? (Plus, I've always held an affinity for words and lyrics, and Rush offered something more in this department than your typical rock band. They were deep thinkers with entire album sides devoted to epic sci-fi, mystical tales created around the interplay between the heart and mind, between authorities and subjects, between kings and the populace.)

At that time in my life, I had a girlfriend who suffered under the weight of my lyrical passions, subject to every chance I could get to win her over to the genius of Peart's multilayered prose. She was surely more amused than amazed at my newfound talent for poetic interpretation. She was patient, listened, often smiled, and encouraged me in my zeal. Little did I know that God was setting the stage for an even greater revelation of the written word.

After yet another one of my music appreciation classes with her as my sole student, she paused, then looked at me and offered, "Tell you what, I'll continue to listen to your interpretation of the words of Rush, but can I share with you some words that are important to me, words that have changed my life?" I agreed. (Only fair, right?) I had no idea what she was about to share. She brought out this thick book, bound in leather, with the words "Holy Bible" inscribed on the cover. Inside were sentences preceded and followed by little numbers; some sentences were colored red and there were footnotes on every page. There were many books within the book. I was surprised and a little intrigued.

After flipping through it to acclimate me to its contents, she turned to a particular place in the old section entitled, "Psalms." She said this was a songbook, containing lyrics of profound meaning about God and to God from several writers, mainly from a king by the name of David. Within Psalms, she flipped to chapter 68. Inside the chapters were many verses, all numbered. She gently slid the book closer to me and asked me to read verse 5. She said it was about God.

I read aloud: "A father of the fatherless . . . "

I stared in silence at the words for what must have been fifteen minutes. Was this the same distant, uncaring God that I was accustomed to? He calls Himself a Father? Especially to people like me? The fatherless? Something stirred within me. The words were right there.

"It's all true," Cathy said. "All of it."

That moment was the spark that lit the flame of a lifelong relationship with God, His Son Jesus Christ, and the gift of the Holy Spirit that will forever reside in my heart. And as I continued to read and study the words in the Bible, I came to experience—to know—how active and full of life and energy His words really are.

Every day since the first time I read Psalm 68:5, I have come to know the reality and love of God who has become my real Father, and how His Word reinforces continually within every page that He is a *good* Father, *attentive* Father, and that He loves us and will never forsake us.

||||||||||||||||||||||||||||||||||||||||||||||||||||||||||||||||||||||||||||||||||||||||||||||||

"The Lord is like a father to His children,
tender and compassionate to those who fear Him."
~ Psalm 103:13, NLT

||||||||||||||||||||||||||||||||||||||||||||||||||||||||||||||||||||||||||||||||||||||||||||||||

The Permanence of His Love

*"For I am certain that nothing can separate us from His love: neither death nor life, neither angels nor other heavenly rulers or powers, neither the present nor the future, neither the world above nor the world below—**there is nothing in all creation that will ever be able to separate us from the love of God which is ours through Christ Jesus our Lord.**" (Romans 8:38–39, GNBDC, emphasis mine)*

Love is more powerful than angels and other heavenly beings, who—created by God—operate in a realm and level of power we cannot fathom. Love is more powerful than two other elements created by God that lie far beyond human reach—time and space. Neither time nor space can even attempt to block the rushing current of His love that is available to us.

And yet, as I read this amazing promise, I have difficulty grasping the magnitude, let alone conveying the immensity of it to anyone else through my writing. His love is hard to grasp and is as vast as angels and heavenly beings and time and space. I feel like theologian A.W. Tozer must have felt when he wrote, "We must try to speak of His love. All Christians have tried, but none has ever done it very well. I can do no more justice to that awesome and wonderful theme than a child can grasp a star. Still . . . as I stretch my heart toward the high, shining love of God, someone who has not before known about it may be encouraged to look up and have hope."

There is so much mystery in love. You can't touch it, but you can feel it. The worth of real love is beyond measure yet doesn't cost a dime. You can receive it, but you cannot keep it, for love was meant to be shared; it requires reciprocity to live and thrive. Love is akin to the manna God fed the Israelites in the desert with—it's miraculous, fulfilling, sustaining—and yet cannot be hoarded. Love, once received, is meant to be given away. If all you do is receive love and never love back, it'll function like the Dead Sea, which receives fresh water, but since it has no outlet, becomes stagnant, a place where sediment grows. If all you do is give love without receiving love, then the well of your heart will dry up. But a love that receives and gives, with love flowing in and out, is like the Sea of Galilee, alive and vibrant, and refreshing. It's the sustenance of manna, giving us the strength and vitality to love others.

True love does not attach itself to selfishness or ulterior motives. It doesn't come with baggage. In its rawest form, true love is a simple giving of oneself to another. We make love complicated when we tag it with conditions as we give it away, those conditions serving the purpose of a sort of return receipt—our attempt to ensure we get something back. This behavior may stem from a lack of reciprocity in the past.

With humans, love will be imperfect, incomplete, and, at best, inconsistent, because we are not the right source. God is the source and if we've blocked the flow of His love then we have only our own limited wells to draw from. As we just read in Romans 8, nothing can separate us from His love. Yet we filter that verse through the broken relationships in our lives and many examples of how human attempts at love create wedges between us and others, then have a very difficult time believing that God is any different. Perhaps the greatest challenge we face as followers of God is in living the truth that we are loved, that God calls us beloved and would go to any length to show us and continually supply us with it if we'd just open up our hearts to Him.

Earlier, Paul says, "Can anything ever separate us from Christ's love? Does it mean he no longer loves us if we have trouble or calamity, or are persecuted, or hungry, or destitute, or in danger, or threatened with death?" (Romans 8:35, NLT) And the answer in verse 37: "No, despite all these things, overwhelming victory is ours through Christ, who loved us."

There's no situation where you could accurately state, "God doesn't love me anymore." Regardless of what you've done or what you're experiencing (even if you feel like He's punishing you because you did something wrong), the truth is He loves you with an unwavering, resolute, steadfast love:

> *"For the mountains may depart and the hills be removed, but my steadfast love shall not depart from you, and my covenant of peace shall not be removed," says the LORD, who has compassion on you." (Isaiah 54:10, ESV)*

"The steadfast love of the LORD never ceases; his mercies never come to an end; they are new every morning; great is your faithfulness." (Lamentations 3:22–23, ESV)

"Steadfast love" in the original language translates to the desire and zeal for showing goodness, kindness, faithfulness, mercy, and favor. From God, not only do these desires for you never cease, they are renewed—fresh—every morning!

There is no way to distance yourself from God's love. Try and run, but it will always be there. His love is inexhaustible, and it doesn't fade or diminish or disappear. Nothing we experience will get in the way; His love is in all, through all, over all. God is the source of love. He created it. It's the true essence of who He is.

The Priority of His Love

Love is more important than the gifts of speaking, prophecy, understanding, knowledge, faith, benevolence, giving, and sacrifice. Love outranks every good virtue ever mentioned in God's Word.

We learn this in Chapter 13 of 1 Corinthians, in my opinion the most famous and thorough text on the topic of love to be found anywhere. Whatever we say, do, think, or act upon is meaningless without love. We are nothing without love in our minds, hearts, and actions. There are just three things that will last forever: faith, hope, and love; and we are told that "the greatest of these is love" (1 Corinthians 13:13, ESV).

The original Greek root for the word "greatest" is *megas*. Whenever we wish to convey something as bigger than big, something of colossal proportions, the largest order of magnitude, we use the word *megas*. Likewise, love is the "*mega*s" of all things that will last forever. Nothing can destroy it; nothing can diminish it. Nothing can usurp its place as number one. The apostle Paul spoke about the superiority of love in his letter to the Colossians. He wrote,

> *"God loves you and has chosen you as his own special people. So be gentle, kind, humble, meek, and patient. Put up with each other, and forgive anyone who does you wrong, just as Christ has forgiven you. Love is more important than anything else. It is what ties everything completely together"* (Colossians 3:12–14, CEV).

Clearly, there is nothing more important or enduring than love. It is the virtue that should permeate every cell in the believer's body, for it's the true essence of God—"God is love" (1 John 4:8, NKJV)—and we are commanded to love precisely because "love is of God" (1 John 4:7, NKJV). So we learn that God is love, and love is of God. It is so paramount that we are commanded to "do *everything* in love" (1 Corinthians 16:14, NIV, emphasis mine). Not some things, but everything.

To summarize, true love—God's love—is constantly with us and in us. It is steadfast and strong and will never leave. And, we are called to share this love. For this to happen, we must be able to tap into an endless, inexhaustible source. That source is God. He is the Creator of it, Supplier of it, Sustainer of it, Replenisher of it. The beauty of His love is that we do not have to plead for it. He gives us His love, freely and without limit.

To love others, you must settle on the fact that God loves you, period. No matter what. And, to know that love is priority number one.

As we wrap up the first part of our *Beloved* Be-Attitude, think about Christ's unwavering love in your own life. When you close your eyes and open your heart to Him, do you feel it? Do you feel His embrace? He is calling you by name. He is wrapping you in His arms. He loves you personally, deeply, and endlessly.

In Part Two of the *Beloved* Be-Attitude, we will focus on the many ways God reminds us of His love in the Scriptures. He uses authors throughout the New Testament—as well as His disciples through the Holy Spirit—to remind us that we are esteemed, favored, and worthy of His love.

BENEDICTION

"The grace of the Lord Jesus Christ, and the love of God, and the communion of the Holy Spirit be with you all. Amen."
(2 Corinthians 13:14)

How has this Be-Attitude encouraged you?

_____

_____

_____

_____

_____

What are some positive actions you can take after learning this practice?

_____

_____

_____

_____

_____

What are you experiencing as you acknowledge God's unending love for you?

_____

_____

_____

_____

_____

CHAPTER 6

*Be*loved

Part 2: Our Love for Others

||||||||||||||||||||||||||||||

"Jesus replied: 'Love the Lord your God with all your heart and with all your soul and with all your mind.' This is the first and greatest commandment. And the second is like it: "Love your neighbor as yourself." All the Law and the Prophets hang on these two commandments.'"
~ Matthew 22:37–40, NIV

"As the Father loved Me, I have also loved you; abide in My love. If you keep my commandments, you will abide in My love, just as I have kept My Father's commandments and abide in His love."
~ John 15:9–11, NKJV

O ur Lord, as well as New Testament authors and great men of faith like Paul, Peter, James, John, Luke, and Jude, called the believers of their time—and they call us today—"beloved." Throughout Scripture we are constantly reminded, by inspiration of the Holy Spirit, how we are seen as esteemed, favored, dear, and worthy of love. Paul singled out eleven individuals in six of his letters, calling them beloved. They were men and women of diverse cultures and callings: a slave, bishop, physician, laborer; they were of mixed heritage: of Asiatic descent, a Persian. God loves everyone, and we are all called into His family by this inexhaustible love. The Bible gives us many examples of believers demonstrating God's love to others.

Love for Each Other

I believe love is the lesson we're being taught in every experience we have. It's the takeaway in every encounter, the wisdom to be gleaned from every situation. If life could be boiled down to one or two questions, perhaps the first would be, "Have I allowed God to love me?" and the second (as a result), "Have I loved others?"

The psalmist said to God, "Your constant love is better than life itself, and so I will praise you. I will give you thanks as long as I live. I will raise my hands to you in prayer" (Psalm 63:3–4, GNBDC). His love permeates everything and everyone who allow His love in.

The apostle Peter writes about the importance of honoring each other in relationship and instructs us on the attitude we should have:

> *"To conclude: you must all have the same attitude and the same feelings; love one another as brothers and sisters, and be kind*

and humble with one another. Do not pay
back evil with evil or cursing with cursing;
instead, pay back with a blessing, because
a blessing is what God promised to give you
when he called you.." (1 Peter 3:8–9, GNBDC)

Love one another—this is the attitude that we're instructed to have in every relationship. When we realize that God loves us continually, forever, then we will learn to love ourselves. After this, we'll be fully capable of loving others with the love He gives us.

||||||||||||||||||||||||||||||||||||||||||||||||||||||||||||||||||||||||||||||||||||||||||||||||||||||||||||||||||||||||||||||

"Let everything you do be done in love [motivated and
inspired by God's love for us]."
~ 1 Corinthians 16:14, AMP

||||||||||||||||||||||||||||||||||||||||||||||||||||||||||||||||||||||||||||||||||||||||||||||||||||||||||||||||||||||||||||||

From God's love and blessing, we're called to bless one another. The word "blessing" in the original language is *eulogia* (Strong's G2129); from it, we get the word "eulogy"—to speak or write high praise or commendation of another. This word is most often associated with funerals, but Peter calls us to "eulogize" the living, to speak praise to others every day, and to honor them with our words.

Love: There isn't a situation where it's acceptable for it to be excluded. Even if we're hounded by our enemies? We should love them (Luke 6:27, ESV). It's the remedy to impatience, envy, jealousy, self-seeking, conceit, cursing, evil, and lies. Try anything else in place of love to fix these ills and it will fail. Love, however, never fails (1 Corinthians 13:8, NKJV).

To love is to truly live. God is love. God is life. And with Him, with love, life is an adventure. It's wild, it's risky, and it's worth it.

In love, we must be transparent. Love is all or nothing. Anything less than total love is a fraud. Love cannot hide some parts and reveal others. We can't fake it, nor can we succeed in love with halfhearted effort. Anyone on the receiving end of that will sniff it out for its lack of authenticity. True love is raw, completely open, all-in, whole, not partial. It's scary, but it's real. True love is not a player. True love is sincere and genuine.

In Christ we are chosen by name, personally invited into a relationship with Him, then shown favor and honor. He set this pattern for relationships in love, a living example of how we should be to others, as Paul stated, "regarding no one from a human point of view" (2 Corinthians 5:16, NIV). We see the world with spiritual lenses, both favor and honor—no condemnation, no separation—just love. We love others through a personal relationship (aka we "know them by name") and then we show them honor (respect) and favor.

Practical *Behaviors* for Experiencing and Sharing God's Love

- After you've been still with God, letting go of any initial worries and concerns that may have hit you that morning, as you open your heart while you quietly sit before Him, open yourself to His love. Say, "Lord, I know You love me, no matter what. Thank you for Your love." Sit and bask in the love He longs to show you.
- Our earthly relationships are not a mirror image of our relationship with God. His love toward us is far greater than our best relationship here and He, in no way whatsoever, is even close to a reflection of our worst one. God is not absent just because our dad was. God is not harsh and controlling just because a former boss was. God is not unpredictable and moody just people around us might

be. God's love cannot be compared to the often-flawed attempts by man. Since we are all works in progress, we have not learned yet how to love completely and unconditionally. And that's okay. God's love, however, is perfect, complete, and not lacking in anything or in any way. And He will show us how to love, but we have to give Him our time and attention.

- Love is not something God wants to throw our way as we zoom by; it is not "drive by" or "drive through"; love is presence. Love is all about connection and relationship, and good relationships are investments of time and attention. The strength of love is in the cultivation of it. It has to be tended to. God spoke this to the prophet Hosea when He said, "I want your constant love, not your animal sacrifices. I would rather have my people know Me than burn offerings to Me" (Hosea 6:6, GNBDC). In the *Be* Still Be-Attitude we learned how much God knows us. In *Beloved*, God wants us to know Him, and as we come to know Him we learn experientially like the apostle John did that God is love. So, let's put down our offering (anything that substitutes for our presence), and instead, let's give Him our time and attention.

- As we meditate on God's love for us, the Holy Spirit will give us names of people and prompt us to pray for them. In the process, He may show us how to act in love toward them. Love, ultimately, proves itself in action. John referred to himself as "the Apostle Jesus loved." He did not doubt where he stood with Jesus in that department, and he had this to say about that love: "Dear children, let's not merely say that we love each other; let us show the truth by our actions" (1 John 3:18, NLT).

- Our love toward others is proof that we belong to Christ; He said so to His disciples, and us today: "So now I am giving you a new commandment: Love each other. Just as I have loved you, you should love each other. Your love for one another will prove to the world that you are my disciples" (John 13:34–35, NLT). How will the world know we are Christ's disciples? By our acts of love. Let's think daily of at least one unsolicited act of love that we can show someone, then do it! Let's write these actions in our journal, along with how God works in them.

- Let's remind ourselves of these three things: the presence of God's love, the permanence of God's love, and the priority of God's love. He loves us continually, forever, and more than we could possibly imagine!

- Let's close with what Paul said to the church in Philippi to accentuate the importance of putting His Word into our minds in order to love well. In an upcoming Be-Attitude, *Be*lieve, we'll explore further the importance of His Word for our lives, but for now, a prayer:

> *"So this is my prayer: that your love will flourish and that you will not only love much but well. Learn to love appropriately. You need to use your head and test your feelings so that your love is sincere and intelligent, not sentimental gush. Live a lover's life, circumspect and exemplary, a life Jesus will be proud of: bountiful in fruits from the soul, making Jesus Christ attractive to all, getting everyone involved in the glory and praise of God." (Philippians 1:9–11, MSG)*

As we allow ourselves to be loved by Jesus, let's picture His love enveloping our spirits, minds, and bodies with inexhaustible, radiant light. Imagery is important: His Word is filled with it. Let's see in our minds the bright beams of light carrying His love and flooding our entire being with it. Next, we'll explore the fourth Be-Attitude, **Beam**, where His light illuminates within us, revealing His character and His desire to expose and eliminate the dark things we tend to hide. He wants us to be holy, pure, and filled with His glory; and He does this by developing lightness and transparency in our character, on the way to becoming more like Him.

"And may the Lord make you increase and abound in love to one another and to all, just as we do to you."
~ 1 Thessalonians 3:12, NKJV

||||||||||||||||||||||||||||||||||||||||||||||||||||||||||||||||||||||||||||||||||||||||||||||||||||||||||

YOUR *BEA*CON: Beloved Basics (2+ minutes)
- God is love. Continue in quiet meditation, reminding yourself of God's deep, infinite love for you.
- Contemplate whom you'll serve in love today, and how.

||||||||||||||||||||||||||||||||||||||||||||||||||||||||||||||||||||||||||||||||||||||||||||||||||||||||||

*BE*NEDICTION

"The grace of the Lord Jesus Christ and the love of God and the fellowship of the Holy Spirit be with you all." (2 Corinthians 13:14, ESV)

||||||||||||||||||||||||||||||||||||||||||||||||||||||||||||||||||||||||||||||||||||||||||||||||

God turns our . . .
Fear into Love
Trouble into Joy
Worry into Peace
Testing into Patience
Selfishness into Kindness
Pride into Goodness
Despair into Faithfulness
Angst into Gentleness
Lust into Self-Control

||||||||||||||||||||||||||||||||||||||||||||||||||||||||||||||||||||||||||||||||||||||||||||||||

How has this Be-Attitude encouraged you?

_____

_____

_____

_____

_____

What are some positive actions you can take after learning this practice?

_____

_____

_____

_____

_____

What are you experiencing as you acknowledge God's unending love for you?

_____

_____

_____

_____

_____

CHAPTER 7

*Be*am

||||||||||||||||||||||||||||

"You are the source of all life, and because of your light we see the light."
~ Psalm 36:9, GNBDC

"Arise! Shine! Your light has come; the LORD's glory has shone upon you. Though darkness covers the earth and gloom the nations, the LORD will shine upon you; God's glory will appear over you. Nations will come to your light and kings to your dawning radiance."
~ Isaiah 60:1–3, CEB

When I was young and needed to be awakened every weekday morning for school, my mom would come into the bedroom that my two brothers and I shared, flick the light switch on, and sing, "Rise and Shine!" Back then, my adolescent self-dreaded hearing that, for it meant another day of classes. But now, whenever I hear the words of Isaiah 60—"Arise! Shine!"—I remember Mom's attempt to infuse positive words of hope into our young minds. It was just one of the many ways in which she worked to instill optimism in us, and I look back now with great appreciation for that—not the waking up part, but the spirit in which my mom helped us begin our day.

Isaiah had the same intent—speaking positive words to dissipate the gloom because a new hope was coming, a light for the nations that would carry with Him God's glory to shine upon us and remove the darkness.

Isaiah had spoken words like this to the people already. In chapter 9, he pronounced, "The people who walked in darkness have seen a great light; those who dwelt in the land of the shadow of death, upon them a light has shined" (Isaiah 9:2, NKJV); and a few verses later he connects this statement with one of our most familiar Christmas passages, saying, "For unto us a Child is born, Unto us a Son is given; and the government will be upon His shoulders. And His name will be called Wonderful, Counselor, Mighty God, Everlasting Father, Prince of Peace" (Isaiah 9:6, NKJV). That Son, that Prince of Peace and Great Light, is Jesus Christ.

Through the presence of Christ, we are exposed to and infused with positive energy. We radiate the beautiful rays of His essence, His glory upon us. We are made light through His spirit. In the light, everything is exposed. God desires that we live transparently, authentically, and sincerely. Darkness is sin; in it lie secrets, shame, and separation. Living in His light is freedom, belonging, purity, and righteousness. Thankfulness, appreciation, gratitude, and kindness are all rays within His light, exposing us to an eternal realm that transcends the negative forces of this world. He is the Light of the world. He offers us His light, that we might become light and be light for others. Goodness, kindness, and mercy are light, emanating from their source—Jesus Christ.

The Opposite of Light

But we have an enemy, and he is darkness. As King David cries to God, "the enemy pursues me, he crushes me to the ground; he makes me dwell in the darkness like those long dead. So my spirit grows faint within me; my heart within me is dismayed" (Psalm 143:3–4, NIV). The good news coming from this otherwise dreary discourse is what David says next, a proclamation that can only flow out of an intimate relationship with God.

He knows the remedy when darkness starts to cast a shadow over his heart: "I remember the days of long ago. I *meditate* on all your works and consider what your hands have done. I spread out my hands to you; I thirst for you like a parched land" (verses 5–6, emphasis mine). David meditated on God's works, remembering His goodness; many of which he recorded in Psalms and what we find elsewhere in Scripture. But we can also meditate on the good works God has done in our own lives. We can remember all of the ways in which we have experienced God's love and favor.

We've all spent time in the darkness. Whether physically or spiritually, when we are in darkness, we cannot see. The darkness is disconcerting, so much so that our very first and immediate inclination is to search for light. We need light.

But we're not excluded from dark times. Death is darkness; depression is darkness. So are loneliness, fear, and hatred. And as long as the devil has a grip on this world, disaster and devastation and evil will cast shadows and lurk in the alleys. But here's the promise of light: clouds may block the sun, but the sun never goes away. We may "walk through the valley of the shadow death," yet we "will fear no evil; for You are with me; Your rod and your staff, they comfort me" (Psalm 23:4, NKJV).

As Winston Churchill once advised, "If you're going through hell, keep going." Christ assures us that, with Him, we will not stay in the dark. Notice too—it's the valley of the *shadow* of death. You cannot have a shadow without light. Even in our darkest times, light is there to guide us. The light of Christ upon you will throw the shadow behind you as He guides you through even the darkest times. The guarantee for the believer is that the light of Christ will overtake the darkness. In John 1:4–5 (GNBDC), we read, "The Word [Christ] was the source of life, and this life brought light to humanity. The light shines in the darkness, and the darkness has never put it out." Darkness can never put out the light! In Christ, we have everlasting light! I'm sure you have experienced a moment in the midst of using a flashlight when the batteries died—always a frustrating experience (especially if you don't have fresh batteries around!). In Christ, you never have to worry about the light going out!

The solution for darkness is light. They cannot coexist. Light always overcomes the darkness. He is the true Light: "God is light; in Him, there is no darkness at all" (1 John 1:5, NIV). And, if "we walk in the light, as He is in the light, we have fellowship with one another, and the blood of Jesus, His Son, purifies us from all sin" (verse 7).

God, the Creator of the universe, spoke light into being from the darkness: "Then God commanded, 'Let there be light'—and light appeared. God was pleased with what he saw. Then he separated the light from the darkness, and he named the light 'Day' and the darkness 'Night.' Evening passed and morning came— that was the first day" Genesis 1:3–5, GNBDC). He understands both darkness and light; in fact, no one understands it better than

He, the Creator of it. Through this awareness, the psalmist confesses to God, "I could ask the darkness to hide me or the light around me to turn into night, but even darkness is not dark for you, and the night is as bright as the day. Darkness and light are the same to you" (Psalm 139:11–12, GNBDC).

In this Be-Attitude, God's light will reveal what lies in the dark recesses of our minds and hearts as He illuminates every corner of our being. There is no condemnation in the light, only grace, and freedom. We receive His pure light as we continue in stillness and meditation, envisioning the purity and warmth of it, which purifies us. His light reveals what lies hidden in our own personal darkness. When things which we've tucked away in the dark recesses are revealed, He deals with it, and through His spirit, we are counseled and made whole. In the *Be*am Be-Attitude we practice humility, resisting pride by having hidden sins revealed and released to Him while seeking restoration and renewal:

> *"All who do evil hate the light and refuse to go near it for fear their sins will be exposed. But those who do what is right come to the light so others can see that they are doing what God wants." (John 3:20–21, NLT)*

As believers, we should want anything that may hinder our walk with Him to be exposed. Since we know that God loves us, we can bring out anything we've suppressed and stored in the dark parts of our soul to His light, knowing that He will lovingly work to remove that from our lives and heal us: "There is therefore now no condemnation for those who are in Christ Jesus" (Romans 8:1, ESV). As believers, we know that God will not shame us. He will not guilt us or condemn us for our sins. He will restore us! He desires that we are made whole, complete.

Light amidst Pain

David always seems to find the remedy to his pain through the process of pressing into God and crying out to Him. Through his sorrows and his musings on the purpose of man's short life, in both moments of victory and defeat, David always finds himself back in the presence of God, the beginning and the end, the Alpha and Omega.

We find this throughout the Psalms. In the following one, Psalm 39:4–7 (NKJV), David continues to struggle with shame and grief and seems to be at the lowest point of his life, enveloped in darkness. I get the sense in reading this that he's not even sure he can carry on. Where do we run to when we fail ourselves and others do too, both inevitable acts in our short existence on this planet?

> "LORD, make me to know my end, and what is the measure of my days, that I may know how frail I am. Indeed, you have made my days as handbreadths, and my age is as nothing before You; certainly every man at his best state is but vapor. Selah. Surely every man walks about like a shadow; surely they busy themselves in vain; he heaps up riches, and does not know who will gather them. And now, LORD, what do I wait for? My hope is in You."

There will be times of darkness, the shadows creeping over our lives. We'll feel small, insignificant, as we struggle against the pressures of life. Life, for a time, will seem fleeting. But we have hope! We have a light! We can be calm, still, and quieted when we know the source of hope, which is God. Everything comes back to Him. So David knew as he prayed through his pain that, rather than worrying or striving, that waiting was the answer. I recently came across a Swedish proverb that states, "Worry often gives a small thing a big shadow."

We need the light of Christ to place perspective on our problems, which often aren't nearly as big as we make them out to be. And we tend to enlarge them the longer we wait for relief, for answers. God wants us to see the blessing in waiting. The Hebrew meaning of the word "wait" is "to endure with strength and expectation." It's an engaged, active waiting full of anticipation for the answer just up ahead, and we can confidently expect God to be there for us in any circumstance, especially in trials. It may seem like nothing is happening in the waiting, as our circumstances remain the same. Know that God is actively at work in these times. Continue to seek Him, to seek His light, and press into Him.

> "You were once darkness, but now you are light in the Lord, so live your life as children of light. Light produces fruit that consists of every sort of goodness, justice, and truth. Therefore, test everything to see what's pleasing to the Lord, and don't participate in the unfruitful actions of darkness. Instead, you should **reveal** the truth about them. It's embarrassing to even talk about what certain persons do in secret. But everything exposed to the light is **revealed** by the light. Everything that is **revealed** by the light is

light. Therefore, it says, 'Wake up, sleeper!
Get up from the dead, and Christ will shine
on you.'" (Ephesians 5:8–14, CEB, empha-
sis mine)

This is yet another reminder of my mom's encouraging wake-up call. Wake up, sleeper! Arise and shine! Christ is here to shine on you!

It's God's light shining in us and through us that distinguishes the believer from everyone else, and it's what should attract others to Him. From His light come all the virtues that we are to shine on to others.

There is a special person in my life who has been a continual light to me: my brother Dan. The light that comes from him is truly amazing. When I think of light, I think of energy and the warmth coming from it; I think of the positive. Dan embodies all of these qualities. You will always find yourself feeling better after you've spent time with him. God has gifted him with the ability to encourage; he's an eternal optimist. He simply favors people and his modus operandi is kindness. He is a walking benediction. People love being around him because he makes everyone feel loved. He doesn't strive to shine. It's not work to him. He simply receives the light of God in faith and it shines out to everyone around him.

That's the beautiful thing about spiritual light. We cannot manufacture it. It's not ours to create. It's simply ours to receive. No striving, just acceptance. And when we allow our hearts to be flooded with the true light—the light of Christ—then that light, which knows no boundaries, will inevitably shine from our hearts to others. Here's an excerpt from one of my journals that I believe accentuates this thought:

"Be a light as much as you can be light. You cannot create light for others. Do not try. You can only be light to shine on them. They can either accept this or turn away. If they accept My light that shines through you, then I'll continue a work in them. You alone cannot. Don't worry about this. Let Me take this. Open your heart to Me. Be open to receiving My light, and be open to releasing it. That is all you can do. That is all you have to do."

How freeing is that?!

I think of churches and their sanctuaries adorned with stained-glass windows, beautiful works of art comprised of scenes and shapes in a multitude of colors. These gorgeous windows are like the lives of God-seekers present in the heart of God: His sanctuary. We are His workmanship, shaped piece by piece, transparent, and framed in Technicolor®. In and of themselves, these windows are magnificent, and stunning, even on the cloudiest of days. But their true beauty, in which the windows display their ultimate magnificence and glory, is when the light shines through them. We, like these windows, have been made to shine His light on a dark world.

"You yourselves used to be in the darkness, but since you have become the Lord's people, you are in the light. So you must live like people who belong to the light, for it is the light that brings a rich harvest of every kind of goodness, righteousness, and truth."
(Ephesians 5:8–9, GNBDC)

"You are the light of the world. A city that is set on a hill cannot be hidden. Nor do they light a lamp and put it under a basket, but on a lampstand, and it gives light to all who are in the house. Let your light so shine before men, that they may see your good works and glorify your Father in heaven." (Matthew 5:14–16, NKJV)

Notice how the verse doesn't say to create your own light and then make your light shine. It says "*let* your light shine"—the light that has been given to you by the true source of light. Any good work we do stems naturally from having received Him; we are simply encouraged to get out there and not hide the light we've been given. Psalm 34:4–5 (ESV) says: "I sought the LORD, and He answered me and delivered me from all my fears. Those who look to him are radiant, and their faces shall never be ashamed." As we seek Him, we turn to Him. All that we need to do is simply turn around and look to Him. That's it—just turn your face toward your Deliverer. He will shine His light on you. Receive Him like you receive the sun.

C. S. Lewis said, "I believe in Christianity as I believe that the sun has risen: not only because I see it, but because by it I see everything else." By the light of Christ, we see everything else, and His light is dependable, just as the sun rises every morning. When we want to feel the warmth of the sun, we turn our faces toward it. There is little effort and zero striving in that endeavor. The only action we're required to take is to step out into it and face it. Same with God. Do you want to shine His light? Then step into Him and turn your face toward Him. We start this in the *Be* Still Be-Attitude.

In Psalm 34:5, the root word for "radiant" is multi-faceted. Primarily, it's translated as "to sparkle," and "to shine and give light." But it goes beyond that because it's often used in the context of happiness, so it's further defined as "to be glad and rejoice, from the light or brightness of a happy face." There's an additional element to this word, too, as described further in Strong's translation of Hebrew: " . . . be cheerful; hence (from the sheen of a running stream) to flow, i.e. (figuratively) assemble: flow (together), be lightened" (Strongs H5102).

I love the idea of God's light flowing through us, creating in us a cheerful radiance: "Then you shall see and become radiant, and your heart shall swell with joy" (Isaiah 60:5, NKJV), ". . . and their faces shall never be ashamed." The shame described here is of arising from disappointed hope, wherein one blushes from confusion, from being confounded. All of that melts away in the presence of His light. His light radiates hope and clarity.

As we receive His light, exposing the dark corners where we've hidden things in our souls, we first repent for our sins committed against Him. Next, if we have any pain that we've experienced through any hardship resulting in bitterness, anger, or sorrow, we release these feelings to Christ. Lastly, after confession (repentance) and release of our hurts and burdens, we proclaim our renewed hearts—purified by His love and power. This can and should be a daily practice as we receive His light, to:

Repent   Release   Renew

Practical *Be*haviors for Living in the Light

- Let's begin seeing situations from the vantage of whether they bring light into our life (as defined in God's Word) or darkness. Read Jesus' preaching on "the lamp of the body" in Luke 11:33-36 (NKJV) and pray for wisdom in taking heed and discerning the light from the darkness.

- Pray for guidance in this area. God will make plain to us what is the true light. Prayer is a conversation with God: simply talking with Him about this.

- Understand that light is an inside job: "For God, who said, 'Let light shine out of darkness,' has shone in our hearts to give the light of the knowledge of the glory of God in the face of Jesus Christ" (2 Corinthians 4:6, ESV). God will do a work in us; from our hearts, He will cultivate love as we see Him and understand who He is and His glory reflected in the person of Jesus.

- Read His Word daily, continually, to discern what's true (light) and false (darkness). Here's why: the devil disguises himself as an angel of light. But he is a liar. If we know the Truth, if we know Jesus Christ, revealed in His Word and through a personal intimate relationship with Him, then the lies and deception from the enemy will be clearly discerned, for his ways cannot stand the light. And he can never be light, he can only put on the disguise and masquerade as if he were in the light. As the apostle John wrote, "The darkness is passing away, and the true light is already shining" (1 John 2:8, NKJV).

- Let's journal our experiences in this area, writing down "Light" moments. Let's document when we've experienced God's light and times when His light became light for someone else. We'll start to see a pattern of light and goodness. We'll be drawn more and more to the true Light and will develop a passion to live there.

- Before making decisions about what to think or how to act, let's cultivate the practice of asking ourselves if we'd like for it to be exposed to the light, for all to see.
- Let's commit to living as persons of light, trusting in God to act on our behalf.
- We should cultivate the disciplines of repenting, releasing, and renewal.

||||||||||||||||||||||||||||||||||||||||||||||||||||||||||||||||||||||||||||||||||||||||||||||||||||

YOUR *BEACON*: Beam Basics (3+ minutes)
- Envision the light of Christ shining on you, through you.
- Allow His light to expose the dark thoughts and feelings of your heart. Repent of them.
- Release to Jesus any wrongs made against you.
- Envision your whole being flooded with light.
- Thank God for renewing you. Shine His light to others!

||||||||||||||||||||||||||||||||||||||||||||||||||||||||||||||||||||||||||||||||||||||||||||||||||||

BENEDICTION

The Lord gave Moses a blessing to have the priests, Aaron, and his sons, speak over the children of Israel, one I find to be an appropriate benediction as we close this Be-Attitude:

> *"The LORD bless you and keep you;*
> *The LORD make His face shine upon you,*
> *And be gracious to you;*
> *The LORD lift up His countenance upon you,*
> *And give you peace."*
> *(Numbers 6:24–26, NKJV)*

How has this Be-Attitude encouraged you?

_____

_____

_____

_____

_____

What are some positive actions you can take after learning this practice?

_____

_____

_____

_____

_____

Imagine Christ's light flooding every corner of your heart. What would He see? How would you respond to Him in what He exposed?

_____

_____

_____

_____

_____

> "I ask that your minds may be opened to see
> His light, so that you will know what is the
> hope to which He has called you, how rich
> are the wonderful blessings He promises to
> His people, and how very great is His power
> at work in us who believe. This power work-
> ing in us is the same as the mighty strength

which He used when He raised Christ from death and seated Him at His right side in the heavenly world." (Ephesians 1:18–20, GNBDC)

||||||||||||||||||||||||||||||||||||||||||||||||||||||||||||||||||||||||||||||||||||||||||||||||

Will we open up the doors
to the sanctuary of our hearts
Where the Lord resides?
Will all be welcome
to worship there
Where Christ's light shines,
and nothing hides?
Will they feel the warmth of the Son beaming through
our stained-glass eyes,
color casting on the rows;
where His love light finds
The altar of our souls?
This—the cathedral of our lives
Holding service in all our days—
Can they join the choir in our hearts
Singing joyful songs of praise?

||||||||||||||||||||||||||||||||||||||||||||||||||||||||||||||||||||||||||||||||||||||||||||||||

Now let's venture on to the next Be-Attitude, **Believe**, where the light of God's Word will strengthen our faith as we learn how to live as Christ lived.

CHAPTER 8

*Be*lieve

Part I: The Word

|||||||||||||||||||||||||||

"But these have been written in order that you may believe that Jesus is the Messiah, the Son of God, and that through your faith in Him you may have eternal life."
~ John 20:31, GNBDC

So, there's the cadence: we read His written Word. We believe. Our faith grows. We experience the fullness of life. Of course, we do not live out a formula, but John 20:31 is a profound statement regarding what happens when we incorporate God's living Word into our lives. It should flow naturally from our connection with Him, open to receiving His holy, inerrant Word, which is life itself. And once we've received His Word, we're drawn closer and will connect with Him on a deeper level. Knowing His Word will provide us with faith, wisdom, truth, and power. It affirms us and gives us the strength to live in victory, from a position of hope and faith and love. His Word confirms who He is, giving us hope that does not disappoint.

Seeing the Bible as God's journal, His love story to us, we're filled with His insight, revelation, and guidance; and when we carry His Word in our hearts, we carry His wisdom and strength, which enables us to face any circumstance and overcome all adversity. In the *Be*lieve Be-Attitude, we reinforce our faith and fortify our belief in all that He says He is and does through His holy Word. We focus on Scripture—the very words of God—to instruct us on how to live well in an otherwise broken world.

||||||||||||||||||||||||||||||||||||||||||||||||||||||||||||||||||||||||||||||||||||||||||||||||||||

"The more you read the Bible; and the more you meditate on it, the more you will be astonished with it."
~ Charles Spurgeon

||||||||||||||||||||||||||||||||||||||||||||||||||||||||||||||||||||||||||||||||||||||||||||||||||||

Christ is the eternal Word. John 1:1–3 (NLT): "In the beginning, the Word already existed. The Word was with God, and the Word was God. He existed in the beginning with God. God created everything through him, and nothing was created except through him."

Christ is the embodiment of the Word. He's so completely connected to it that we're told that's who He is—He is the Word! If you have Jesus, you have the Word. If you have the Word, you have Jesus. Without Him, without the Word, we'd have nothing. With the Word, we have life and light, and unfailing love and faithfulness: "The Word became human and made his home among us. He was full of unfailing love and faithfulness" (John 1:14, NLT).

His faithfulness makes it possible for us to live by faith. The astounding part of having and living out God's Word, whether we read it silently and meditate on it, recite it out loud for others to hear, sing it, or contain it within a prayer, is this: it is living and powerful (Hebrews 4:12 NKJV). His Word is alive! He is alive! The word "living" in the original language, Greek, is *zao* (*zah*-oh), which means "to live, breathe, be among the living (not lifeless or dead); to enjoy real life; true life worthy of His name; active, blessed, endless in the kingdom of God."[6] The word "powerful" in the original language is *energes*. God's holy Word is energy!

Because His Word is infused with life and energy, it's also filled with action and purpose. With every word you take in, God puts His Word to work. Knowing this should increase both our time in it and our faith. He declares in Isaiah 55:10–11 (CEV): "Rain and snow fall from the sky. But they don't return without watering the earth that produces seeds to plant and grain to eat. That's how it is with my words. They don't return to me without doing everything I send them to do."

The purpose of rain doesn't end after it hits the ground. God uses the water to accomplish many wonderful things for the purpose of creating and growing. A seed, when planted, dies, then with new life, it germinates into plants for food. God's Word doesn't just sit on a page. When we read it, it becomes implanted in our spirit, and it creates life, meaning, and purpose with exponential impact. It instigates renewal in our hearts and out of it,

---

6 "G2198 - *Zaō* - Strong's Greek Lexicon (NKJV)." Blue Letter Bible. Accessed February 5, 2022. https://www.blueletterbible.org/lexicon/g2198/nkjv/tr/0-1/.

creates beautiful things in us and others. Things spiritual. Things leading to creation and change and growth.

Meditate on His Word

> *"Finally, brethren, whatever things are true, whatever things are noble, whatever things are just, whatever things are pure, whatever things are lovely, whatever things are of good report, if there is any virtue and if there is anything praiseworthy— meditate on these things. The things which you learned and received and heard and saw in me, these do, and the God of peace will be with you." (Philippians 4:8–9, ESV)*

Paul encouraged the Philippian brothers and sisters earlier in his letter to "join in imitating me, and keep your eyes on those who walk according to the example you have in us" (Philippians 3:17, ESV). In God's Word, we have numerous examples of those we can learn from and emulate in our daily walk.

Belief is strengthened by learning (by meditating on His Word) and by putting into practice what we learn.

> *"Every scripture is inspired by God and is useful for teaching, for showing mistakes, for correcting, and for training character, so that the person who belongs to God can be equipped to do everything that is good." (2 Timothy 3:16–17, CEV)*

As we learn Scripture, He equips us to do good. Scripture reveals our character, then it refines it. Like the dross that's skimmed off the top from heated silver, Scripture serves to bubble up the impurities in our life, so that they might be skimmed off as He purifies our hearts. The silversmith knew the silver was finally pure when he could see his reflection in it. God's Word, like silver, reflects His character and we become a reflection of Him as we grow by living in His Word. By the inspiration of the Holy Spirit, as we remain in His Word, we'll learn to want what He wants: "But if you remain in me and my words remain in you, you may ask for anything you want, and it will be granted!" (John 15:7, NLT).

Jesus is the embodiment of the Word, so naturally, as we remain in Him, His words will remain in us. And as we follow Him, He instructs us and teaches us in the way we should go.

The Shepherd and His Sheep

Reading through the Bible, we're led out on a quest to find truth, wisdom, and love. And there is a great emphasis on setting out in the proper way, as followers of Christ (versus leaders of self!). He leads us.

"Trust in the LORD with all your heart and lean not on your own understanding; In all your ways acknowledge Him, and He shall direct your paths" (Proverbs 3:5–6, NKJV). He is the director of our way; it's His path we're on. "Acknowledge" means to know. Jesus said, "and the sheep follow Him because they know his voice. But they will never follow a stranger; in fact, they will run away from him because they do not recognize a stranger's voice" (John 10:4–5, NIV).

In those days, there were many shepherds and many sheep, and they typically all comingled in the same pen. But, when it was time to go, the shepherds called their own flocks and only those who belonged to that shepherd responded, following their shepherd. We are the sheep of our good Shepherd Jesus, and to follow Him we must know His voice, otherwise, we'll mistakenly respond to the other voices calling out. And, one of the primary ways we come to know the voice of our Shepherd is through His Word: "Let me hear of your unfailing love each morning, for I am trusting you. Show me where to walk, for I give myself to you" (Psalm 143:8, NLT). There's a connection to knowing His Word and hearing His voice, for Scripture cries out and He speaks through His holy Word. "I've wandered off like a sheep, lost. Find your servant because I haven't forgotten your commandments!" (Psalm 119:176, CEB).

Virtually every story in God's Word is about someone's journey, about their pilgrimage. Much is written about walking, running, riding, sailing, building, et cetera, but it's more about the inner journey of our spirits and who we become in the process of relationship. Acts 17:28 NKJV) says, "In Him, we live and move and have our being." God compels us to act as He leads and guides us. In Plan A, we play the role of the "captain of our souls," orchestrating every thought and moving from the limited reservoir of our own capabilities. In *Plan Be*, we rest in Him, pray and fellowship with Him, meditate on His Word, then act on what God does as the true Captain of our souls, obedient to the leading of the Holy Spirit through the endless well of eternal and beautifully good possibilities. Yes, it's that easy.

*BE*NEDICTION

"Most assuredly, I say to you, he who hears My word and believes in Him who sent Me has everlasting life, and shall not come into judgment, but has passed from death to life."

(John 5:24, NKJV)

How has this Be-Attitude encouraged you?

_____

_____

_____

_____

_____

What are some positive actions you can take after learning this

_____

_____

_____

_____

_____

How has God's Word encouraged you in your journey?

_____

_____

_____

_____

_____

CHAPTER 9

*Be*lieve

Part 2: Faith

IIIIIIIIIIIIIIIIIIIIIIIIII

"Therefore, having been justified by faith, we have peace with God through our Lord Jesus Christ, through whom also we have access by faith into this grace in which we stand, and rejoice in the hope of the glory of God."
~ Romans 5:1–2, NKJV

J esus came to seek and save the lost. His love and the love of His Father compelled Him to do so. He did the work to reconcile us to God so we wouldn't have to.

If you were to obtain eternal life through your own effort, then, how would you do it? How would others do it? At what point would a person's efforts be lacking, versus yours? Who would get to decide what level of effort is good enough? Who sets the standard? Only God can set the standard, for there is no one greater. When Jesus came to save us, He sacrificed His life so that we might live. This is grace. If we can accept this grace, then we'll surrender ourselves in faith that not only did He save us so that we might live eternally with Him, but that we no longer have to work and scrape and push and pull to earn His favor. We are accepted. Just believe. No doing this or that, simply faith.

In accepting God's grace, we live in right standing with God; no earning, therefore, no boasting. It's the difference between working for wages and receiving a gift. He gave us a gift.

The Scripture says, "Abraham believed God, and God counted him as righteous because of his faith" (Romans 4:3, NLT). Those who work are paid wages, but the wages are not regarded as a gift; they are something that has been earned. But those who depend on faith, not on deeds, and who believe in the God who declares the guilty to be innocent, it is this faith that God takes into account to put them right with Himself. This is what David meant when he spoke of the happiness of the person whom God accepts as righteous, apart from anything that person does: "Happy are those whose wrongs are forgiven, whose sins are pardoned! Happy is the person whose sins the Lord will not keep account of!" (Romans 4:3–8, GNBDC).

This truth is reinforced by Paul again, in his letter to the Galatians:

> "Yet we know that a person is put right with God only through faith in Jesus Christ, never by doing what the Law requires. We, too, have believed in Christ Jesus to be put right with God through our faith in Christ, and not by doing what the Law requires. For no one

is put right with God by doing what the Law
requires." (Galatians 2:16, GNT)

The bottom line is this: To simply *believe* is the only requirement by God to be right in His eyes, accepted, eternally forgiven,
and a child whom He welcomes into His kingdom, now and forever. But we don't believe in a program or a system. We believe
in a person: Jesus Christ. He's the one who made it possible to
have eternal life. Jesus came to this earth to seek and save the lost.
He sacrificed His life to save yours and mine. As written in John
6:28–29, CEV, "God wants you to have faith in the one He sent."
That person is Jesus Christ.

Faith Is the Foundation

Once you believe in the Jesus who saves, that He alone is the
reason that we will never die, then we can move on to another
aspect of faith that is vital for the believer—a faith that is progressive. The more we come to know Jesus, the more our faith in Him
will grow. We come to know Jesus more by spending time in His
Word—by hearing it, reading it, speaking it, singing it, et cetera.

So, as we practice the *Believe* Be-Attitude, we need to get
straight on the relationship between faith and works. Faith is foundational. It's the bedrock on which all other virtues and works sit.

The old legalistic system says, "I do, therefore I am," but those
in Christ say, "I am, therefore I do." It becomes a question of who
you believe is really doing the work. If you think it's you, then
you will have a performance-based mindset, thinking of how you
might work to do what He does, to gain His favor, to earn a right
to be called His disciple. But if you believe in Christ, then you'll
believe He is the work of God. And if He is the work of God, then

your perspective shifts to one of obedience. You will listen to Him and you will learn that being precedes doing.

Jesus was approached by a centurion who desperately pleaded for the healing of his servant who was back at his home, paralyzed and in great agony. Jesus was, as always, willing. He even offered to come to the centurion's home. What the centurion said next greatly impressed Jesus. The centurion said, "Lord, I don't deserve to have you come under my roof. Just say the word and my servant will be healed" (Matthew 5:8, CEB).

When Jesus heard this, he was so impressed that He said to the people following him, "'I say to you with all seriousness that even in Israel I haven't found faith like this.' Then Jesus said to the centurion, 'Go; it will be done for you *just as you have believed.*' And his servant was healed that very moment" (Matthew 8:10,13, CEB, emphasis mine).

Could it be that our life rises to the level of our belief? Perhaps that's what we need to attend to rather than all our efforts and striving. We study, sweat, labor, and strive to act in a way as to position ourselves favorably, get ahead, win first place, be seen as the best, and stand on top of the podium. But according to Jesus, belief is the real driver. Belief moves mountains, not brute strength or force.

|||||||||||||||||||||||||||||||||||||||||||||||||||||||||||||||||||||||||||||||||||||||||||||||||||||||||||||||

> *"Some trust in chariots and some in horses,*
> *but we trust in the name of the Lord our God."*
> ~ *Psalm 20:7, ESV*

|||||||||||||||||||||||||||||||||||||||||||||||||||||||||||||||||||||||||||||||||||||||||||||||||||||||||||||||

Once we have professed our belief in the saving power of Jesus Christ, He takes us on a journey that will continually grow our faith. He wants us to remain strong in our belief in His continual presence and power in our lives. We have an enemy, though—the devil, who, once we've accepted Christ as Lord, will do everything he can to reduce our faith. He'll try to get us to doubt and eventually, completely disbelieve Christ and His work in our hearts. It's an epic spiritual battle, one that we've already won since we've been given eternal life, but nonetheless, the enemy will continue to try and kill our faith.

Battling Unbelief

A desperate father sought help from the disciples to cast out a demon that possessed his son. When Jesus arrived on the scene, the father said to Him, "'But if you can do anything, have compassion on us and help us.' 'What do you mean, "If I can"?' Jesus asked. 'Anything is possible if a person believes'" (Mark 9:22–23, NLT).

I imagine the weight of those words hanging in the air as Jesus said them. I picture Jesus staring intently into the father's eyes as the words sunk deep into the man's broken heart. Words for him alone. And now a word for us today. The word "is possible" in the Greek is *dynamos*, and its root word is *dynamai*—like dynamite.[7] Power. Belief is Power.

And the Father's response? The same one we'd have, in light of the countless pain-filled, helpless ordeals he must've recalled at that moment as he watched his child once again convulsing on the ground. As we witness another tragedy. As we get struck down by

---

7   "G1415 - *dynatos* - Strong's Greek Lexicon (NLT)." Blue Letter Bible. Accessed February 5, 2022. https://www.blueletterbible.org/lexicon/g1415/nlt/mgnt/0-1/. And "G1410 - *dynamai* - Strong's Greek Lexicon (NLT)." Blue Letter Bible. Accessed February 5, 2022. https://www.blueletterbible.org/lexicon/g1410/nlt/mgnt/0-1/.

sickness. As we too watch helplessly while loved ones around us suffer: "I believe; help my unbelief!" (Mark 9:24, ESV).

He will help our unbelief. Jesus' response after that man's comment is key. Jesus could've said, "Oh, so you don't believe. Never mind," and then walked off. But Jesus is not that person. Jesus is a healer, full of mercy and compassion all the time. What He did next was to heal the boy. Jesus knows our fears and doubts. He understands through His own experience on this earth how hard life can be, how much we're surrounded by pain and turmoil. And He acts despite all of the things which we might use to disqualify ourselves from His grace. On more than one occasion, he called out His disciples' lack of faith, but He never abandoned them. He remained faithful, even unto death, having returned to His disciples and gifting them—and us—with the presence of the Helper, the Holy Spirit. So just as the father was ministered to once he brought his son to Jesus, we'll be when we come to Him. Unbelief is rooted in distance. But Christ hasn't bolted. He's always present.

It's so reassuring that we serve a God who lived on planet Earth. He experienced all of the joys and struggles and relationships and responsibilities we face. He can relate deeply with whatever we're going through and He calls us to Himself with compassion to come and learn: "Come to Me, all you who labor and are heavy laden, and I will give you rest. Take My yoke upon you and learn from Me, for I am gentle and lowly in heart, and you will find rest for your souls. For My yoke is easy and My burden is light" (Matthew 11:28–30, NKJV).

Tucked in the middle of this passage, in between Jesus' promises of rest, is a key to unlock the secret to true belief. It answers the question we've all surely asked Him at one point: "Okay, Jesus, I've come to you. Here I am. Now what?" Jesus' answer is the key: *learn from Me*. The more we learn from Him, the more we become strengthened in our faith. Belief replaces unbelief. But how do we learn from Him? We come to Him, yoke with Him, we talk with Him (pray) and we study His Word. As we read His Word, we're taught how to hope. The Scriptures encourage us on our journey:

> "Everything written in the Scriptures was written to teach us, so that we might have hope through the patience and encouragement which the Scriptures give us." (Romans 15:4, GNBDC)

The Lord has much to teach us and we have much to learn. Life can be complex, and we need to know how to navigate and overcome it. But we cannot do it alone. We need a relationship with One who can guide us through it all—and not just to guide, but to help us thrive. Through His Word, we receive patience to deal with life's issues and hope to fuel our purpose.

God didn't just create us, send His Son to save us, then just walk away and leave us to figure things out on our own. As a Teacher (Jesus was called this often by His followers, in the Hebrew as "Rabbi"), He longs to instruct us, guide us, and counsel us upon the best path for our lives. But Jesus is infinitely more than a teacher. He holds on to the position of Lord, our King, with not only the passion to instruct, but the power (that biblical word *dunamai*!), like a king would, to make it happen! His will be done! The deep knowledge that He possesses and longs to share with us is experiential. We are not following someone who never walked in our shoes. Let that sink in for a moment. Jesus is not a statue or a religious concept—He is a real person, one who stepped on the same soil as man and faced the same hardships. He laughed, He shed tears, He collaborated, and He confronted.

He held our hands. He looked us in the eye. He communicated directly with us. And now He sits at the right-hand side of God in heaven's throne room as one who can intimately identify with us.

Also, in Him, we have a High Priest who is able to sympathize with our weaknesses. In the original language, the word "sympathize" means to "experience with": He's walked in our shoes. And in doing so He made it possible for us to walk in His:

> *"Now that we know what we have—Jesus, this great High Priest with ready access to God—let's not let it slip through our fingers. We don't have a priest who is out of touch with our reality. He's been through weakness and testing, experienced it all—all but the sin. So let's walk right up to him and get what he is so ready to give. Take the mercy, accept the help." (Hebrews 4:14–16, MSG)*

And now, as One seated at the right hand of our Father in heaven, He holds the position of interceding on our behalf to bring our lives in line with His kingdom, to empower us with all of the spiritual blessings in the heavenlies while we journey through this world. He holds all of the secrets and mysteries of the universe. His curriculum is astonishing! His classroom is full of glory, wisdom, power, and grace. When we realize what He knows and how He longs to guide and instruct us, how could we not desire to sign up for His class? "Oh the depth of the riches both of the wisdom and knowledge of God!" (Romans 11:33, NKJV).

Practical *Be*haviors for Cultivating the *Be*lieve *Be*-Attitude:

- An important part here is to see how God connects the dots between any insight or revelation we've received during *Be* Still, *Be*loved, *Be*am, and *Be*lieve. God will!
- Know and remember that the purpose of *Be*lieve (and its corresponding Liberty, Learn) is to come to better know our Lord and Savior Jesus Christ. It's not for book smarts, it's not knowledge for knowledge's sake. Scripture has many stories and countless lessons that we can draw from to improve our lives, but the main point is that Scripture reveals a Person—Jesus—who longs to have a relationship with us.
- Thanks to our modern-day, app-driven society, there are several excellent resources we can download. Here are a few Bible apps which provide daily Scripture verses and offer devotionals in just about every translation imaginable:
- *YouVersion*—the preeminent and must-have Bible app. And it's free! It includes daily devotional and Bible study plans from many spiritual teachers ranging from one day to one year and based on various life topics (love, hope, anger, stress, relationships, learning the Bible, et cetera). We can schedule YouVersion to automatically text message the verse of the day before our morning quiet time (https://www.youversion.com/). I find the daily verse to be a great start to spending time with God every morning and reflecting on that verse all day.
- *Blue Letter Bible*—I use it for reading commentaries from respected scholars and translating words into the original languages, which provides great insight into the meaning of words and phrases. It's free but they do take donations.

- *Bible Hub*—Another devotional that includes a robust commentary section from many spiritual teachers, as well as a dictionary of Bible themes and words. Free.
- *Abide*—Audio prayers based on, like YouVersion, a multitude of topics (subscription-based).
- Let's pray for wisdom. Pray for it often. There is nothing more important than wisdom. "But if any of you lack wisdom, you should pray to God, who will give it to you; because God gives generously and graciously to all." (James 1:5, GNBDC).
- Let's make Proverbs and Psalms a regular part of our learning time. These books are packed with wisdom, practical advice, encouragement, and, yes, tough (and constructive) love.
- Whenever we hear, read, pray over, write down, speak, sing, or reflect on His Word, let's remember that it is living and active. It's difficult to fathom, but it's true—His Word is alive and carries with it a purpose almost beyond comprehension! And whenever we read, He acts. We should remember Isaiah 55:11—that His Word never returns void—and enjoy the amazing privilege of being part of this extraordinary work.
- "Be careful how you think; your life is shaped by your thoughts" (Proverbs 4:23, GNT). And our thoughts come from whatever it is we decide to let into our minds. Let's fill our minds with Scripture, and then we'll be better able to think rightly.

We're ready to move from *Be*lieve to the next Be-Attitude—*Be* Joyful. God's presence, His love, His light, and His Word are each cause for great celebration and the type of joy that distinguishes believers from everyone else in the world.

||||||||||||||||||||||||||||||||||||||||||||||||||||||||||||||||||||||||||||||||||||||||||||||||||||||||||||||||||||||

YOUR *BEACON*: Believe Basics (5 minutes)
- Time for a Bible verse! Read one. Write it down.
- Contemplate it. Study it. Commit it to memory.
- Pray over this verse for insight on how to apply it.

||||||||||||||||||||||||||||||||||||||||||||||||||||||||||||||||||||||||||||||||||||||||||||||||||||||||||||||||||||||

*BE*NEDICTION

*"Now may the God of hope fill you with all joy
and peace in believing, that you may abound
in hope by the power of the Holy Spirit."
(Romans 15:13, NKJV)*

How has this Be-Attitude encouraged you?

_____

_____

_____

_____

_____

What are some positive actions you can take after learning this practice?

_____

_____

_____

_____

_____

Write down and commit to memory one Bible verse that encourages you.

_____

_____

_____

_____

_____

CHAPTER 10

Be Joyful

Part 1: Joy

||||||||||||||||||||||||||||

"Be joyful always, pray at all times, be thankful in all circumstances. This is what God wants from you in your life in union with Christ Jesus."
~ 1 Thessalonians 5:6–18, GNBDC

When we continually see God at work, in us and around us, and come to know experientially the freedom He offers through Christ, then the door is opened for a life of joy and celebration. We can live as free-spirited, contented people not through some artificial or externally driven means, but by the irrevocable promise of His care and love. He will never leave or forsake us, and He will always work to the good for those of us who love Him. His consistency, His continual presence, His honesty, and unending love should be the catalysts for a happy life. We are free to laugh, sing, think positively, and not be controlled by circumstances:

> *"But as for me, I will sing about your power.*
> *Each morning I will sing with joy about your*
> *unfailing love. For you have been my refuge,*
> *a place of safety when I am in distress."*
> *(Psalm 59:16, NLT)*

We can opt for joy in every circumstance because He has ensured us that we will experience the best outcome we could ever ask for—eternity with Him. Because of His promise of everlasting life with Him, we live with hope, and hope fills us with joy. We can experience this even in times of distress. I understand how difficult this can be in the day-to-day grind, but that doesn't eliminate the fact that we can still find joy. We always have the power to create joyful moments, for ourselves and others. More specifically, we can implement those things which we know bring joy.

When I'm feeling down, I decide to open the book of Psalms. God's Word is filled with encouragement. I decide to listen to a song that cheers me up. I go to a segment on YouTube of inspirational messages that I've bookmarked for occasions like this. I launch into podcasts I've subscribed to, from those I know serve as a bright light to others' lives. I exercise regularly. I run. These are my preemptive strikes against the sadness and doldrums. The point is, we can implement practices that serve to lift us out of the ditch—or, better yet, keep us out to begin with. The psalmist declared that he'd sing songs every morning about God's unfailing love. That's a decision, friends, to stave off the lurking shadows of "anti-joy" trying to creep into our lives.

But the reality of life is that there will always be darkness, depression, tragedy, accidents, and ultimately death. Christ knows this. He lived on this earth. He died a violent death; He felt emotional and physical pain. He was ignored, ridiculed, and betrayed. The thanks He received for bringing all of the love and healing to us was to be hunted down, a bounty on His head. He was continually on the run and had no stable place to lay His head. Despite all this, He conquered death. He defeated the darkness. And He encourages us with these words: "I have said these things to you, that in me you may have peace. In the world you will have tribulation. But take heart; I have overcome the world" (John 16:33–34, ESV).

We serve an Overcomer, One who has experienced all of the anti-joy that we do, yet came out victorious. So take heart, He is reaching out with both hands to lift you up. There is joy for us.

||||||||||||||||||||||||||||||||||||||||||||||||||||||||||||||||||||||||||||||||||||||||||||||||||||

Joy is the serious business of Heaven.
~ C. S. Lewis

||||||||||||||||||||||||||||||||||||||||||||||||||||||||||||||||||||||||||||||||||||||||||||||||||||

Good Grief

You may find it strange that I'm bringing up the topic of grief in the *Be* Joyful Be-Attitude, but the ability to stay content always, especially in difficulties, is, I believe, one of the surest marks of a mature Christian, a powerful testimony to our faith, and one of the most compelling ways that others will be drawn to God.

Francis Ward Weller wrote a beautiful passage on the relationship between (and need for) gratitude and grief, and in it perhaps we can catch a glimpse of what God is up to in allowing both in our lives.

> *"The work of a mature person is to carry grief in one hand and gratitude in the other and to be stretched large by them. How much sorrow can I hold? That's how much gratitude I can give. If I carry only grief, I'll bend toward cynicism and despair. If I have only gratitude, I'll become saccharine and won't develop much compassion for other people's suffering. Grief keeps the heart fluid and soft, which helps make compassion possible."*

A joyful, contented life is not one where we smile through the pain, or somehow ignore it altogether, pretending to be okay. Remember, love must be sincere. Many times, we're not okay, and that's okay! A truly joyful life embraces both difficulties and blessings and trusts God in both, knowing that He will produce in us resiliency and confidence as we triumphantly overcome. Think about the most real, authentic person you know. I'm willing to bet you think of them in this manner because they live out their lives salted with encouragement and positivity, yet seasoned with the groundedness and wisdom that comes through adversity. The attractiveness of such a person is in seeing how they've pressed into God and through His strength risen above the tragedies and defeats to remain content. My siblings in the Hanrahan clan—Lori, Sue, Jim, and Dan—work from this core of optimism, and at the same time we declare that a Hanrahan always gets back up again. Yes, we may get knocked down, but we will not be defeated. We will always get back up again.

We just read Jesus' declaration that we will experience tribulation (John 16:33, NKJV). If we allow it, grief can be a very effective tool in bringing us to the end of ourselves. And it isn't until we reach the point of surrender that we can receive from the only One who can help—God. A.W. Tozer said it well: "The reason why many are still troubled, still seeking, still making little forward progress is because they haven't yet come to the end of themselves."

You see, we cannot complete ourselves, only God can. And if our lives are nothing but rainbows and unicorns then we will never see our need for God. So adversity can be seen as a gift. (I know—this is graduate-level theology! And I'm still learning!) Perhaps the greatest enemy to true spiritual growth isn't pain, but comfort, of being taken care of in every aspect of our lives so that adversity is kept at bay. If we are truly honest with ourselves, though, we'd admit that oftentimes, it's the friction that results in smooth and radiant beauty, like a pearl polished by sand. The good news is that Jesus didn't stop with "In this world, you will have tribulation." He continues on to say, "But *be of good cheer*, I have overcome the world." (John 16:33, NKJV, emphasis mine). Press into the One who has conquered the world and everything that it can throw at you.

I've had several "end of my rope" moments in my life. Being laid off from my job was one example, but it was small in comparison to being told by several doctors that my wife and I would never have children. The news pulverized my dream of becoming a dad. Having grown up without one, I remember praying for children before I even started seriously dating! That's how much I hoped to be a father. Yet today, my heart overflows with gratitude, because as I write this I rejoice in my amazing adult son and daughter. And I rejoice in over three decades of marriage, forged strong by leaning into the storms together while we both trusted our eternal Savior. Our journey to conceive our children took over twelve years. We had devastating moments with seemingly nowhere to turn, but each time God provided a way.

God never says, "You lead, I'll follow." He always paves the way, always before us, leading and guiding. And He never leaves the path. He is always present, lovingly showing us through any dark valley we may have. God ensures that whatever valley we're in, we will not remain there. He will see us through it.

So, joy is always available—and "graduate-level" living is one that can decide to implement joy in any circumstance. We can always declare as King David did in Psalm 9:1–2 (ESV) as he reflected upon God's protection against his enemies and His righteous judgment: "I will give thanks to the LORD with my whole heart; I will recount all of your wonderful deeds. I will be glad and exult in you; I will sing praise to your name, O Most High."

To exult is to jump for joy, which he was able to do after recounting, remembering, all that God had done for him. Let us do the same. And let us particularly remember that in every circumstance, God knows what's going on in every situation and is involved in every aspect of our lives.

||||||||||||||||||||||||||||||||||||||||||||||||||||||||||||||||||||||||||||||||||||||||||||||

> *"The great thing, if one can, is to stop regarding all the unpleasant things as interruptions of one's 'own' or 'real' life. The truth is of course that what one calls the interruptions are precisely one's real life—the life God is sending one day by day." ~ C.S. Lewis*

||||||||||||||||||||||||||||||||||||||||||||||||||||||||||||||||||||||||||||||||||||||||||||||

Turn the Channel

My older brother Jimmy gave me sound advice when we were just little tykes—three brothers sharing one bedroom. I was having what I called "fast dreams" with scenes spinning wildly around in my brain and crashing into each other without end. This continued for what seemed like every night for weeks. I would roll around trying to fight them off, often keeping Danny and Jimmy awake in the process. When I explained to them what was going on—that it was like a bunch of movies and TV shows playing all at once in my brain, Jimmy—who is to this day is a man of few but often profound words, simply said, "Then turn the channel."

That phrase has stuck with me ever since. When I'm hit with bouts of sadness, weighed down by bad news, or struck by adversity, I remember Jimmy's advice and simply "turn the channel." I'm not ignoring the problem, I'm simply remembering instead to tune in to joy—for that station is always on the air. My mind stops the negative program that's running, I step down from the witness stand in my mental courtroom where I'm being judged by the jury of my own angst and fears, and I decide to tap into the endless reservoir of God's love, acceptance, and trust.

Romans 8:6 (NLT) says, "But letting the Spirit control your mind leads to life and peace." I surrender control of my mind to the Spirit and I do this through prayer. And by the way, I haven't mastered it. I'm not sure I ever will, but that's okay. I'm a work in progress and I love who's progressing me. Like Paul, I'm reminded that:

> "I do not claim that I have already succeeded or have become perfect. I keep striving to win the prize for which Christ Jesus has already won me to Himself. Of course, my brothers and sisters, I really do not think that I have already won it; the one thing I do, however, is to forget what is behind me and do my best to reach what is ahead. So I

> *run straight toward the goal in order to win the prize, which is God's call through Christ Jesus to the life above. All of us who are spiritually mature should have this same attitude. God will make this clear to you."* (Philippians 3:12–15, GNBDC)

Our attitude should be a positive, winning attitude, infused with humility in the reality that we're a work in progress. No one has completely arrived, but we press on, forgetting what's behind us. And we move forward toward the finish line with determination even as we know He'll get us through it. I try to participate in several official, sanctioned running races a year, and when I first signed up for the races, my main concern was crossing the finish line. I did not have the confidence then to be sure of it. Would my legs tire out? Would I run out of gas, not properly hydrated? Would I push myself to injury? I feared seeing "DNF" ("Did Not Finish") next to my name in the race results. But the more I trained and the more races I ran, my concern for finishing disappeared. It was no longer "Will I finish?" but "When will finish?" That's an example of pressing on.

As believers, we have that same confidence. Our journey in this life is a marathon race, run with eyes focused on the finish line and the prize of the "life above," which is heaven. What greater joy can there be in knowing that we will be with Him in heaven someday?! Paul exhorts us to "run with endurance the race that is set before us, looking to Jesus, the author and finisher of our faith" (Hebrews 12:1–2, NKJV). Most likely you've heard of the Boston Marathon. As Christians, we run the "Believers' Marathon." Jesus has already finished the race and He was able to do it "for the joy set before Him, enduring the cross" (verse 2). That joy is us! He endured and finished because He wants us to finish and to "live above" with Him. Paul also refers to Jesus in this passage as the Author of Faith. The Greek word for author is *archegos*, which comes from *arche*, which means "the first person in a series," and the word *ago* which means "to lead by laying hold of, and in this way to bring to the point of destination." Jesus started the race. Jesus finished the race. And He, our eternal Pacer, will lead us through our race and enable us to win the prize of eternity as He leads us across the finish line. With Jesus leading, there is no DNF. We will finish!

|||||||||||||||||||||||||||||||||||||||||||||||||||||||||||||||||||||||||||||||||||||||||||||||||||

*"For the kingdom of God is . . . righteousness
and peace and joy in the Holy Spirit."*
~Romans 14:17, NKJV

|||||||||||||||||||||||||||||||||||||||||||||||||||||||||||||||||||||||||||||||||||||||||||||||||||

Abiding Joy

Jesus spoke to His disciples about the need to remain in Him, illustrating the key to their relationship through the metaphor of the vine and the branches (see John 15:1–8, ESV). Jesus is the Vine, and we are the branches. We must abide in Him, and His words abide in us (*Believe*—Learn!). Apart from Him, we can do nothing. And only in Him—Christ working through us—can we bear fruit—"love, *joy*, peace, patience, kindness, goodness, faithfulness, gentleness, and self-control" (Galatians 5:22–23, NIV, emphasis mine). And Jesus speaks too of abiding in His love (see John 15:9–10, ESV).

Then, after all that Jesus commanded them to do in John 15, He provides the reason: "These things I have spoken to you, that my *joy* may be in you, and that your *joy* may be full" (John 15:11,

ESV, emphasis mine). Jesus is satisfied with nothing less than our fullness of joy. The Greek word for "full" is defined as "filled to the full," "to cause to abound, to furnish or supply liberally."[8]

Joy is the exclamation point in everything Christ says. It is the reason He came and the reason He saved us. But we don't have to wait for the sweet by-and-by for joy to come. We are saved now, and we can have His joy now!

As we wrap up this portion of the *Be* Joyful Be-Attitude, consider the joy quotient in your own life. Are you seeking it through prayer? Do you find joy in knowing your prize—heaven—is at the finish line? Through the Holy Spirit's gentle guidance, are you able to "turn the channel" to find the joy station?

BENEDICTION

"Be glad in the Lord and rejoice, you righteous; And shout for joy, all [you] upright in heart!
(Psalm 32:11, NKJV)

How has this Be-Attitude encouraged you?

_____

_____

_____

_____

_____

8   "G4137 - *Plēroō* - Strong's Greek Lexicon (ESV)." Blue Letter Bible. Accessed February 5, 2022. https://www.blueletterbible.org/lexicon/g4137/esv/mgnt/0-1/.

What are some positive actions you can take after learning this practice?

_____

_____

_____

_____

_____

Write down three things that have given you joy lately, then write a note of thanks to God for them.

_____

_____

_____

_____

_____

CHAPTER 11

Be Joyful

Part 2: Prayer

||||||||||||||||||||||||||

"Rejoice in the Lord always. I will say it again:
Rejoice! Let your gentleness be evident to all.
The Lord is near. Do not be anxious about
anything, but in every situation, by prayer and
petition, with thanksgiving, present your requests
to God. And the peace of God, which transcends
all understanding, will guard your hearts and
your minds in Christ Jesus."
~ Philippians 4:4–7

Our world is spinning faster than ever in a whirlwind of tension and stress. At our frantic pace, we strive to keep up with unrealistic demands, creating a busyness culture focused on performance and recognition. We've worked ourselves sick with anxiety through the cycle of overextension, sacrificing rest for results. Because of this, I believe what so many people are after are peace and tranquility. God's Word provides the remedy in Philippians 4:4–7 above.

These verses are packed with sound advice that will if followed, heal our hearts and provide the peace and tranquility we greatly desire. The very first thing we should do is rejoice. Not just once, or when something good happens, but always. Paul emphasized this point by stating it twice: rejoice!

Next, know that the Lord is always near. Psalm 139:1–9 (GNBDC) says,

> "LORD, you have examined me and you know me. You know everything I do; from far away you understand all my thoughts. You see me, whether I am working or resting; you know all my actions. Even before I speak, you already know what I will say. You are all round me on every side; you protect me with your power. Your knowledge of me is too deep; it is beyond my understanding. Where could I go to escape from you? Where could I get away from your presence? If I went up to heaven, you would be there; if I lay down in the world of the dead, you would be there. If I flew away beyond the east or lived in the farthest place in the west, you would be there to lead me, you would be there to help me."

How often have we been on conference calls, talking away, only to realize after too long that we've been on mute and no one has heard a word we said? Well, with God, He always hears us; there is no mute button with Him! We can pray in confidence that He's always there to hear and understand what we're saying.

After we rejoice and remember that He is near, any anxiety that we still have can be replaced by peace through prayer and thanksgiving. Not only will the prayer and thanks replace the anxiety, it will stand guard over our hearts and minds to ensure anxiety cannot further infiltrate.

Peace: A Simple Formula

Through the combination of prayer and petition (continued seeking and asking) with thanksgiving, we set ourselves up for a positive, rich inner life in fellowship with the Spirit. The result is peace. Not worldly peace, but the eternal peace of Christ. Jesus loves us so much that He didn't stop at giving us the inexpressible gift of saving our souls. He gave us another gift until we meet Him at the threshold of eternity—peace. "Peace I leave with you; my peace I give you. I do not give to you as the world gives. Do not let your hearts be troubled and do not be afraid" (John 14:27, NIV). Only His peace expels trouble and fear.

Peace, as seen in God's Word, can be defined as "the tranquil state of a soul assured of its salvation through Christ, and so fearing nothing from God and content with its earthly lot, of whatsoever sort that is."[9] Tranquility and contentment—don't we all want that? And God shows us how. It's so simple:

---

9   "G1515 - *Eirēnē* - Strong's Greek Lexicon (NIV)." Blue Letter Bible. Accessed February 5, 2022. https://www.blueletterbible.org/lexicon/g1515/niv/mgnt/0-1/.

Praise + Prayer = Peace

Praise is our expression of thanks and awe to God. Prayer is our continual dialogue with Him in the relationship. The result is an intimacy that inevitably results in a heart buoyed by peace.

He informs us that "the mind controlled by the Spirit is life and peace" (Romans 8:6, NIV); He gifted us with the Holy Spirit—our Counselor, our Guide—who, in our surrender, takes over and controls our minds in a state of vitality (life!) and contentment.

Scripture tells us that the Holy Spirit even prays for us when we are at a loss for words:

> *"In the same way, the Spirit comes to help our weakness. We don't know what we should pray, but the Spirit himself pleads our case with unexpressed groans. The one who searches hearts knows how the Spirit thinks because he pleads for the saints, consistent with God's will." (Romans 8:26–27, CEB)*

God has your back! Not only has He given us His own Son Jesus Christ to save us, but Christ in return has given us the Holy Spirit to sustain us until He returns.

What we think about is crucial. Our thoughts are always part of the equation for peace and joy. The apostle Paul shows us how to overcome our anxieties and troubles in Philippians 4:8 (NIV):

> *"So keep your thoughts continually fixed on all that is authentic and real, honorable and admirable, beautiful and respectful, pure and holy, merciful and kind. And fas-*

ten your thoughts on every glorious work of
God, praising him always."

No doubt, he heeded the advice of Solomon: "Be careful how you think; your life is shaped by your thoughts" (Proverbs 4:23, GNT). All of the things to think about in Philippians 4:8 are positive. I'm sure he could've come up with a list of twenty other positive things to think about, but you get the point—there's no room for negativity. It's well understood that as we think, we become. Our actions stem from character, and character from our beliefs. Our beliefs are cemented in by the thoughts which come from, well, whatever we allow in. Very few things in life are obvious. One of those that is, is the reality of darkness and light. We easily know the difference. Another is negative and positive. Many try casting shadows, blurring the lines on right versus wrong. But, if we would admit it, we all know. And what Paul is saying is this: choose to think on the things that we all know are positive. Just as joy can be a choice, so is hatred, bitterness, anger . . . darkness. Choose joy instead! Choose light!

Finding Joy through Prayer

This *Be* Joyful Be-Attitude is one where we express gratitude to God for all we have in Him. And it is also where we focus on our needs and the needs of others through prayer. His will for our lives is that we live always in a spirit of joy and thankfulness, and in close relationship with Him through prayer.

Bill and Patti Johnson are two great examples in my life of living with a spirit of joy and happiness. Gratitude is always on their lips, servanthood is always on their hearts, and the desire to see others blessed is their banner. They have loved me and my family deeply, pouring time and prayers into us continually, championing God's work in our lives, and teaching us how to live in Him and to trust Him with a spirit of thankfulness and contentment. Their selfless service is their joy.

Thanks and prayer. I encourage you to express them daily. As we live thankfully, we remember the good that has come into our lives because of the work of Christ in it. In prayer, we look to the moment and to what lies ahead, yoking with God as it concerns the needs of our lives and those around us. Both are ways that we'll keep the dialogue open with Him. God desires to connect with us continually; He looks for us. As the psalmist declares: "My heart has heard you say, 'Come and talk with me.' And my heart responds, 'LORD, I am coming'" (Psalm 27:8, NLT).

Someone once said that if we could see the very center of a Christian's heart, we would find it always at prayer.
~ *Neil Anderson and Robert Saucy,* The Common Made Holy

Contentment

Another facet of the *Be* Joyful Be-Attitude is contentment. Have you ever noticed that sometimes (if not most of the time), you find yourself sinking away from joy as you compare yourself to others? *My car isn't nice enough. My house isn't big enough. I wish I were thinner. I wish I made more money.* Comparison—and discontentment—are thieves of joy. However, God's Word tells us that "Godliness with contentment is great gain" (1 Timothy 6:6, NKJV).

The biblical definition for contentment is "to be satisfied." A life in God is satisfied with possessing the very basics and nothing more. Paul goes on to explain further in the next verse, "For we brought nothing into this world, and it is certain we can carry nothing out" (verse 7). This verse makes me think of the old saying that we "never see a hearse pulling a U-Haul". There have been many sermons preached on the topic of "You can't take it with you." I also think of another popular saying that "we spend the first half of our lives trying to accumulate things, and the second half trying to get rid of them." Having lived for over half a century, I can proclaim that is true. Certainly, our possessions can possess us; they can become more of a burden than a blessing, with all the work to take care of them.

After having lived for a while on this earth, we realize that true blessings aren't things we can purchase. Love and friendship—these are blessings. Love of money and riches, not so much, according to Paul. Again, 1 Timothy 6:9–10 (NASB):

> *"But those who want to get rich fall into temptation and a snare and many foolish and harmful desires which plunge men into ruin and destruction. For the love of money is a root of all sorts of evil, and some by longing for it have wandered away from the faith and pierced themselves with many griefs."*

Chasing the almighty dollar is a tortuous affair and based on what Paul writes, faith can never be found there, much less contentment and satisfaction, or joy. Thankfully, he provides an alternative, citing the things which will lead to contentment:

> *"But flee from these things, you man of God, and pursue righteousness, godliness, faith,*

> *love, perseverance, and gentleness. Fight the*
> *good fight of faith; take hold of the eternal*
> *life to which you were called, and you made*
> *the good confession in the presence of many*
> *witnesses." (1 Timothy 6:11–12, NASB)*

If we are to hold on to anything, it's the eternal life—a life full of behaviors that in and of themselves have eternal qualities about them, as they can outlive us. When we leave this earth to be at home with the Lord, our loved ones will remember the godliness, faith, love, patience, and gentleness we showed them. Whatever good will outlast us is what we should hold on to here.

Perhaps these are some of the treasures that Jesus encourages us to store up when He says:

> *"Do not lay up for yourselves treasures on*
> *earth, where moth and rust destroy and*
> *where thieves break in and steal, but lay up*
> *for yourselves treasures in heaven, where*
> *neither moth nor rust destroys and where*
> *thieves do not break in and steal. For where*
> *your treasure is, there your heart will be*
> *also." (Matthew 6:19–21, ESV)*

Houses, cars, boats, furniture, golf clubs, musical instruments, clothing . . . none of these are bad to have, and they can temporarily add to the pleasures of living on this planet; but they will undoubtedly decay and rust, or be lost, or worse, or taken from us. Contentment, true satisfaction, and joy are in the things that are not subject to deterioration or limited shelf life. I truly believe that the character and virtues we grow within and share with others will not only continue with us in our spirits as we enter heaven, but will also be left behind for others, as seeds planted in their hearts, as deposits in their treasure chests to bring out and share with others. Lasting joy is in the love and relationships we cultivate here and in the intimacy we have with our Lord. Let us focus on, and be content with, such things. This is how Paul, while imprisoned, was able to say,

> *"Not that I am speaking of being in need, for I have learned in whatever situation I am to be content. I know how to be brought low, and I know how to abound. In any and every circumstance, I have learned the secret of facing plenty and hunger, abundance and need. I can do all things through him who strengthens me." (Philippians 4:11–13, ESV)*

When we focus on Christ, He will strengthen our resolve in every situation. In the experience of His continual presence, we will realize the simplicity of contentment. It's the joy set before Christ as He faced the cross. It's the satisfaction of Christ alone in Paul's life while he sat in prison. It's the boundless strength God gave Habakkuk even though nothing seemed to be going his way when he wrote, "Though the fig tree should not blossom, nor fruit be on the vines, the produce of the olive fail and the fields yield no food, the flock be cut off from the fold and there be no herd in the stalls, yet I will rejoice in the LORD; I will take joy in the God of my salvation. GOD, the Lord, is my strength; he makes my feet like the deer's; he makes me tread on my high places" (Habakkuk 3:17–19, ESV).

Friend, if all we have is God, then we have immeasurably more than we need, for He has given us eternal life. And this should be cause for great joy and contentment!

Practical Behaviors for Infusing Your Life with Joy

- First and foremost, let's always remind ourselves that God is all we need. No matter what situations we face, we can rejoice in the saving grace He gave us, knowing that our lives beyond this life are secured, and unspeakable joy is ours now and forever.

- Let's record moments in our journal that have brought us joy and the things we're thankful for, keeping track of the things that bring positive feelings and make us smile. In the *Plan Be* Journal Template at the end of this book, we provide space to write these down. It is so important to be able to take the time to list out what makes us happy and thankful and to show gratitude to God for what He has given us. Reminding ourselves of the joyous times instills in us a deep hope for the days ahead.

- Let's talk to God—whatever is on our minds and hearts. This is prayer. He is always available and always attentive, listening. He hears our needs, our cries. He wants to commune with us. We should pray for our needs and the needs of others, and pray often.

- Let's write down our prayer needs. Track them and we'll find over time how God answers because He always answers, and we will come to learn His wisdom. This will bolster our faith and love for Him: "Ask, and it will be given to you; seek, and you will find; knock, and it will be opened to you. For everyone who asks receives, and he

who seeks finds, and to him who knocks it will be opened"
(Matthew 7:7–8, ESV).

- In prayer we ask—we make requests. We seek Him, His will. We knock on heaven's door every time we pray, and He gladly opens it and invites us in! He promises we'll receive answers; sometimes it's a no answer (and that's to our benefit, ultimately) but He does promise we will find Him when we seek Him.
- Let's realize, from God's rich storehouse of joy, that He has given us the ability to create joy and laughter; we don't have to wait for someone else to.

Here's a secret when it comes to experiencing joy: rejoicing precedes joy. We don't wait for joy to come before we rejoice in the Lord. We rejoice always and give thanks in all circumstances. Joy will come as we rejoice in Him.

Earlier, in *Be* Still, you listened to God, quiet before Him. You received His love (*Be*loved) and light (*Be*am), preparing to spend time in His Word (*Be*lieve), that it might strengthen your faith. In *Be* Joyful, we encourage you to talk with God. And that's all prayer is—talking with God. It's about seeking Him out and pursuing Him in relationship.

So, *Plan Be*-er, we leave the *Be* Joyful Be-Attitude with a benediction to exercise gladness of heart. It is in us!

||||||||||||||||||||||||||||||||||||||||||||||||||||||||||||||||||||||||||||||||||||||||||||||||||||||||||||||||||

YOUR *BEACON*: Be Joyful Basics (3+ minutes)
- Write down at least one thing you are thankful for and one prayer.
- Think of who you can be a joy-giver to today and write down what you'll do for that person.

||||||||||||||||||||||||||||||||||||||||||||||||||||||||||||||||||||||||||||||||||||||||||||||||||||||||||||||||||

*BE*NEDICTION

"God is the one who makes us patient and cheerful. I pray that He will help you live at peace with each other, as you follow Christ. Then all of you together will praise God, the Father of our Lord Jesus Christ."
(Romans 15:5–6, CEB)

How has this Be-Attitude encouraged you?

_____

_____

_____

_____

_____

What are some positive actions you can take after learning this practice?

_____

_____

_____

_____

_____

Write down the names of three people you can pray for and commit to lifting them up in prayer to God every day.

_____

_____

_____

_____

CHAPTER 12

*Be*hold

||||||||||||||||||||||||||||

"Behold, I stand at the door and knock. If anyone hears My voice and opens the door, I will come into him and dine with him, and he with Me."
~ **Revelation 3:20, NKJV**

The word "behold" is a fascinating word that appears 1,381 times in the King James Bible, 234 times in the New Testament, and four times more often than the word "amen."[10] On its surface, the Greek word for "behold," *idou* (G2400, pronounced ee-*do*), is a verb that means "to see." Per Thayer's Greek Lexicon,[11] it is used in "bidding the reader or hearer to attend to

---

10 "'Behold' in the KJV Bible." BEHOLD IN THE BIBLE. Accessed February 5, 2022. https://www.kingjamesbibleonline.org/search. php?q=behold&bsec=Z&order=0. search for all KJV books
11 "G2400 - *Idou* - Strong's Greek Lexicon (NKJV)." Blue Letter Bible. Accessed February 5, 2022. https://www.blueletterbible.org/lexicon/g2400/nkjv/tr/0-1/.

what is said: 'Behold! See! Lo!'" Thayer's continues to describe the use of the word "behold" as "the simple exclamation of one pointing out something . . . and calling attention."

The word behold is not used in modern speech—when was the last time you heard someone say, "Behold!"? There simply isn't a suitable English word to convey its full meaning and, more importantly, its emphasis. The word itself is a verb—it requires action on the hearer's or reader's part!—and whenever used in a sentence, the speaker or author is making a very strong point to the listener or reader to pay very close attention to what they're about to share. Perhaps today we substitute behold for "Look!" but *Be*hold is much more than that.

"Behold" is also used at the close of a narrative when something new is introduced. It's used when a specific thing is unexpected yet sure; and when a thing is specified which seems impossible and yet occurs. Throughout the Bible, we see this word preface such unexpected events, like:

- the appearance of angels (Matthew 1:20; 2:13; 4:11, ESV)
- wise men (Matthew 2:1, ESV)
- the virgin Mary's being with child (Jesus, Matthew 1:23, ESV)
- the use of hyperbole, like "the log in your own eye" (Matthew 7:4, ESV)
- a great tempest on the sea (Matthew 8:24, ESV)
- a herd of pigs running violently off a cliff (Matthew 8:32, ESV)
- an entire city coming out to meet Jesus (Matthew 8:34, ESV)
- Moses and Elijah appearing to Jesus, Peter, James, and John (Matthew 17:3, NKJV)

"Behold" bookends the Gospels. We first hear it from John the Baptist as he sees Jesus coming: "Behold, the Lamb of God who takes away the sin of the world!" (John 1:29, ESV). And then we see it at the end of Jesus' life, at the cross, when Jesus "saw His mother, and the disciple whom He loved standing by, He said to His mother, 'Woman, *behold* your son!' Then He said to the disciple, '*Behold* your mother!' And from that hour that disciple took her to his own home." (John 19:26–27, NKJV, emphasis mine).

Whenever "behold" is used, we can feel the weight of the word bringing a special emphasis to the text. The NIV version simply states, "Here is your mother," but in other versions, with "*Behold*, your mother," we sense something very special, something new, something profound has occurred, or is about to. Indeed, something glorious did occur, as the resurrected Jesus appeared before His disciples saying, "*Behold* My hands and My feet, that it is I Myself. Handle Me and see, for a spirit does not have flesh and bones as you see I have" (Luke 24:19, NKJV). And in His wonderful proclamation to John in Revelation 1:18 (NKLV), He said, "I am He who lives, and was dead, and *behold*, I am alive forevermore. Amen." There is something magnificent and absolutely beautiful in the beholding!

"Nearness to God brings likeness to God. The more you see God the more of God will be seen in you."
~ Charles Spurgeon

God's in the Details

God can do everything. No purpose can be withheld from Him. The angel said to Mary that nothing is impossible with Him. So then, what are we afraid of? He knows. He sees. He heals the brokenhearted and bandages our wounds. He is larger than life and yet completely attentive to each life that trusts in Him.

We serve a God of great and glorious detail, the One who created entire galaxies and countless species of animals and plants. Everything He does is put on display, for us! We have to desire to look for it, to behold it. Explore, investigate, research, contemplate, engage, search, seek. He entices us, invites us, dares us to step into the arena and play. There are no coincidences. Everything—and everyone—is connected. We just don't see the entire picture, but He does. *Beholding is an invitation to see more than what you're seeing today*, to put new lenses on of expectation that God will show up, and He does! To behold is to toss out the ambivalence and disinterest and, instead, approach life with a sense of wonder, looking for what's hidden in plain sight, knowing that nothing is an accident and that everything has purpose.

The prophet Micah illustrates his approach to beholding: "But as for me, I will look expectantly for the LORD with confidence in Him. I will keep watch. I will wait [with confident expectation] for the God of my salvation. My God will hear me" (Micah 7:7, AMP). As believers, we learn how to look expectantly, with confidence, which is another way of saying *to hope*, and to keep on searching for the Lord, knowing we will find Him. God reinforces this promise through another prophet, Jeremiah, when He says, "You will seek Me, and you will find Me because you seek Me with all your heart" (Jeremiah 29:12, GNBDC), motivated by God's promise in verse 11 that His plans for us are "for peace and well-being and not for disaster, to give you a future and a hope."

(Jeremiah 29:11, AMP). We will find God, whether we see tangible evidence or not. The key is in the seeking.

So, to behold Him is to hope in faith when we cannot see and to rejoice in Him when we can. Either way, we live with adventure in our hearts and a sense of wonder knowing He is always at work in our lives and no experience is ever wasted. Every moment has meaning.

To behold is to live the joy in seeing life from the lens of unbiased observation, to take everything in without judging. We practice the art of observing in a state of "active rest." We are observers for the sake of joy. We are Joy Ambassadors: our mission is to receive it and spread it to everyone He puts us in contact with!

In the *Beam* Be-Attitude, we talked about how we experience God's light. As we live in the light, it goes without saying that we can see much more clearly. It's in the light where we see God at work, blessing us with everyday miracles and opportunities to love others as He does. His desire is that we live with a sense of wonder—in awe of His ways, His beauty, and His love.

The Lord is over all creation. He speaks to us continually through it. He has numbered the stars and calls each one by name. He knows the number of grains of sand in the sea and the number of hairs on your head. His creation, all around us, serves us continual reminders of His love and His promise to take care of us.

If we would really see, we would come to know the depth of His care for us. His created order is one thing. But, it's the unseen beauty of His grace, acceptance, mercy, and the promise of everlasting life through the sacrifice of His Son Jesus Christ that, if we fix our spiritual eyes on it, knowing the work He did for us (work we don't have to do!), we'll realize the true freedom in living and the everlasting provision of His love.

King David declared, "My eyes are always looking to the LORD because He will free my feet from the net" (Psalm 25:15, CEB). He yearned for God and was constantly seeking Him, whether in times of favor or fear. Let us continually look for our Lord!

Welcome Him

The exalted Christ stands at the door of your heart, seeking entrance. Your heart has been closed and at first He is obscured. You only know someone is there after hearing a sound: a knock, was that? Yes! The knock, a summons, followed up by His own voice calling out to you, "It is Me! Allow Me in, that I might dine with you!" So, you stop whatever else you were doing, you make for the door, and open it. And behold! Christ is there!

Notice the first action taken is His. He knocks on your door. He calls out to you. And you simply respond. You open your heart and what follows is a fellowship with Him.

There is simply one prerequisite, one action required on your part: to be attentive. Open your mind, your heart, your senses—your entire being to the possibility that He will come knocking. Be on the lookout! In the Be-Attitude of *Be*hold, we are reminded of Christ's continual involvement in the moments of our day. He is always at your door. If you feel distant, He hasn't moved. Hear Him knocking. We simply have to hear and look. To see and behold. Psalm 11:4 (NKJV) testifies to the Lord's omnipresence: "The LORD is in His holy temple: the LORD's throne is in heaven; His eyes behold, His eyelids test the sons of men."

Now, this may seem strange and disconcerting for the nonbeliever, but it should bring great comfort to the believer, knowing that He is continually attentive. We are to perceive with any and all of our senses how God is working in our lives. God calls us to pay attention, observe, and examine in order to know Him more deeply through His glorious deeds, as certainly He observes and continually attends to us. God is more than just words on a page. He is presence. He is action. We have the ability to see what He is doing and how He is doing it in order to better understand and know Him. We can see Him with eyes of faith:

> *"I pray that he will **give light to the eyes of your hearts**, so that you will understand the hope to which he has called you, what rich glories there are in the inheritance he has promised his people, and how surpassingly great is his power working in us who trust him. It works with the same mighty strength he used when he worked in the Messiah to raise him from the dead and seat him at his right hand in heaven." (Ephesians 1:18–20, CJB, emphasis mine)*

When we live in faith, we are essentially placing trust in the things of Christ we cannot see. For instance, we can't physically see Him, yet we believe He exists. We will find what we are looking for when we look for Christ in and around our lives. We believe in Him and in doing so we believe in love and kindness and goodness and joy and peace—all the things we cannot see. But, when we invite them openly into our lives and act on them, we will see their fruit in the reciprocity of those with whom we share God's love.

> *"Faith is to believe what we do not see, and the reward of this faith is to see what we believe." ~ St. Augustine*

In the *Be* Still Be-Attitude, we discussed how we can sit with calm and ease, and invite our Creator into our day. In the *Be*hold Be-Attitude, we stand, prepared to take hold of the work set before us, with deliberate action and purpose. In *Be*hold, we operate with keen awareness of everything and everyone arounds us, completely engaged in whatever we're doing.

Plan Be is not passive. It is not about driving on cruise control. This is one of the elements that make *Plan Be* unique because, on one hand, it entails full surrender—to Christ our Master—and on the other, full intention and purpose as we live out the life of the believer to positively impact our world. Yes, we are called to both! But we must always remember the priority: being before doing.

||||||||||||||||||||||||||||||||||||||||||||||||||||||||||||||||||||||||||||||||||||||||||||||||||||||||||||||||||

"There are only two ways to live your life. One is as though nothing is a miracle. The other is a though everything is a miracle."
~ Albert Einstein

||||||||||||||||||||||||||||||||||||||||||||||||||||||||||||||||||||||||||||||||||||||||||||||||||||||||||||||||||

The concept of this last Be-Attitude, *Be*hold, is to prepare yourself to walk with God continually, to anticipate divine appointments, or divine "noticing," since nothing is random and life is more than mere coincidence. We approach everything with eyes wide open (spiritually from the heart and physically with our eyes), we regain that sense of wonder that we somehow lost after childhood when everyone told us to get serious and to check into reality and grow up. We need to come back to the spirit of appreciation for the small things, which really aren't small after all.

One of the most famous hymns ever written, and perhaps the most widely sung in church, "How Great Thou Art," was inspired by a sense of wonder. It's based on a Swedish traditional melody and a poem written by Carl Boberg and his experience with the beholding of God in nature:

> "Carl Boberg and some friends were return-
> ing home to Mönsterås from Kronobäck,
> where they had participated in an afternoon
> [church] service. Presently a thundercloud
> appeared on the horizon, and soon lightning
> flashed across the sky. Strong winds swept
> over the meadows and billowing fields of
> grain. The thunder pealed in loud claps.
> Then rain came in cool fresh showers. In a
> little while the storm was over, and a rain-
> bow appeared. When Boberg arrived home,
> he opened the window and saw the bay of
> Mönsterås like a mirror before him . . . From
> the woods on the other side of the bay, he
> heard the song of a thrush . . . the church
> bells were tolling in the quiet evening. It was
> this series of sights, sounds, and experi-
> ences that inspired the writing of the song."[12]

This experience inspired Boberg to pen the opening lyrics: "O Lord my God, when I in awesome wonder consider all the works Thy Hand hath made," which leads up to the chorus:

---

12   Bratt, Wally. "On 'How Great Thou Art.'" Pietisten. Pietisten, Inc., 2002. http://
www.pietisten.org/xvii/2/howgreat.html. Volume XVII, Number 2. Winter 2002-
2003.

"Then sings my soul, my Savior God, to Thee, how great Thou art! How great Thou art! Then sings my soul, my Savior God, to Thee, how great Thou art! How great Thou art!"

Like Boberg, when we live with a sense of wonder, we activate and learn to live the adventure God calls us to live, even in the small things. But what really is wonder? Here are some synonyms:

- Anticipation
- Awe
- Astonishment
- Curiosity
- Fascination
- Hope
- Marvel
- Admiration
- Inquisitiveness

Now, who doesn't want to live out these words in their life? Doesn't it excite you to read these and ask, "How can I cultivate a life that involves these?" The wonder is in giving complete trust to God who guides us. Proverbs 16:9 (ESV) states, "The heart of man plans his way, but the Lord establishes his steps. Jeremiah echoed this when he said, "O LORD, I know that the path of [life of] a man is not in himself; it is not within [the limited ability of] man [even one at his best] to choose and direct his steps [in life]" (Jeremiah 10:23, AMP). As believers, we know we can make our plans yet, ultimately, it's the Lord who directs us according to His divine providence.

Practical Behaviors for How to *Be*hold, to Look:

Here are some ways you can see with spiritual eyes how God is at work continuously around you:

- We realize first and foremost, that God is everywhere. He sees it all and is Lord over all. There isn't a single place where God cannot work. It doesn't matter where we are, who we're with, or what we're doing. God is there. And He's trying to get our attention! "I am a God who is everywhere and not in one place only. No one can hide where I cannot see him. Do you not know that I am everywhere in heaven and on earth?" (Jeremiah 23:23–24, GNBDC).

- Let's know that a major reason why God is in every moment and continually attentive to us is because He cares for us and longs to guide us. He is for us, not against us! He works unceasingly on our behalf!

- Psalm 121 was a song the Israelites sang as they ascended to their festivals in Jerusalem. On their pilgrimage, this song would remind them to look for God and to remember His continual presence and protection. God does not need to sleep; He is always awake and attentive to us. This is a great Psalm to memorize or highlight and bookmark in our bible because we often need this reminder when the going gets tough:

- "I lift up my eyes to the hills. From where does my help come? My help comes from the Lord, who made heaven and earth. He will not let your foot be moved; He who keeps you will not slumber. Behold, He who keeps Israel will neither slumber nor sleep. The Lord is your keeper; the Lord is your shade on your right hand. The sun shall not strike you by day, nor the moon by night. The Lord will keep you from all evil; He will keep your life. The Lord will keep your going out and your coming in from this time forth and forevermore." (Psalm 121:18, ESV)

- Let's remove expectations. It's human nature to force our wants and desire on others, building a set of standards we expect others to live up to, and then we become very disappointed when these expectations aren't met. Let's throw those chains off and be open-minded and accepting of what happens.

- And, more importantly, let's be accepting and loving of other people. If we find ourselves not able to love someone because of some expectation we have standing between us and them of how they should be or live, then we're stopping love in its tracks. We are not the divine ruler and judge of the world, and good news here—we don't have to be! God is. Let Him take that burden away and free us to simply love.

- We can change our lens: Rather than look at happenings in our day from our personal vantage point and their effect on us, we can go into situations with an "others" mindset, remove ourselves from the equation and look at how others are impacted and influenced by what happens.

- Let's live in the moment. We can't truly behold when our minds are farmed out to some future event that may or may not happen, or when stuck on a past event that is no longer a reality. "Now" is the only true place to live. Indeed, "Now" is an eternal, sacred place to live; when we think about it, it's the only mode of time that is timeless! The past ended, the future has yet to be—but "Now" is real, it is here, it is alive!

- Let's be inquisitive and not let experiences blow by us due to a lack of interest, or because they don't fit our agenda, or because we're distracted by living in a past or future plane. Notice the "Now," and take interest in what is of interest to others.

- Think big but see small. Let's remind ourselves that God operates at a level that is unfathomable, that we could never fully grasp the level of power and capability that He has. He knows every detail. Let's realize that if God created it all (and He did!), then He is aware of every detail behind it. Acts 17:24 (NKJV) tells us, "God, who made the world and everything in it, since He is Lord of heaven and earth, does not dwell in temples made with hands."

- God works through people to accomplish His works. If we always look for a "burning bush" moment or miracle outside of human contact, we may miss out on how He is trying to reach us through the person standing right at our side. Yes, God speaks through His creation, like a beautiful sunset, or through other created lives like our pets, but God made us in His image and it's entirely reasonable, and logical, to think that most often he'll speak to us through our relationships with other people—believers and nonbelievers alike.

- We can record God-given moments and experiences in a journal. We just might see a trend in these recorded times, that, if pondered individually, might not make much sense but taken together, will. I believe that one of the mysteries of life lies in the connectedness of things, which can be so easy to overlook. Let's make it a game, an adventure to try and correlate experiences, people, and things to discover a pattern, commonality, or some form of connection. Sometimes there won't be. No harm, no foul! But when, through discovery, we make a connection, it brings such Technicolor to life!

- Beholding is not the end of intimacy with God; on the contrary, it's just the beginning of a continually lasting and deep encounter with Him. Beholding opens the lid to the treasure chest of our hearts. It makes available to us the opportunity of storing up treasures of faith, which we'll be able to access in times of adversity, or in times when we are called to minister to others.
- Lastly, let's be fully present and deliberately checked into our moments. This will require putting aside all potential distractions, like that swipe-able device in our hands!

||||||||||||||||||||||||||||||||||||||||||||||||||||||||||||||||||||||||||||||||||||||||||||||||||||||

YOUR *BE*ACON: Behold Basics (2+ minutes)
- Resolve to face this day with eyes and heart wide-open, with curiosity and a sense of wonder. God says, "Behold! I am doing a new thing!" (Isaiah 43:19, ESV).
- Enter into situations anticipating God at work. Write down your observations.
- Review the past beholding moments. Look for connections.

||||||||||||||||||||||||||||||||||||||||||||||||||||||||||||||||||||||||||||||||||||||||||||||||||||||

*BE*NEDICTION

"Behold, the eye of the Lord is on those who fear Him, on those who hope in His mercy."
(Psalm 33:18, NKJV)

How has this Be-Attitude encouraged you?

_____

_____

_____

_____

_____

What are some positive actions you can take after learning this practice?

_____

_____

_____

_____

_____

Write down some ways in which you can cultivate a life of beholding.

_____

_____

_____

_____

_____

YOUR *BE*ACON: PLAN BE SUMMARY

||||||||||||||||||||||||

BREATHE

- Find a comfortable, quiet place to sit.
- Invite Jesus into your heart.
- Take a deep breath in (allow your stomach to expand).
- Let a deep breath out (stomach contracts).
- Repeat three times.
- If you have time, continue but in a slower, smoother fashion for two more minutes.

BE STILL

- As you sit quietly, pray, "I am here Lord. I am listening."
- Simply remain silent. Allow His Spirit to guide you.
- Re-center with a sacred word if needed (e.g., "peace").

BELOVED

- God is love. Continue in quiet meditation, reminding yourself of God's deep, infinite love for you.

- Contemplate whom you'll serve in love today, and how.

BEAM
- Envision the light of Christ shining on you, through you.
- Allow His light to expose the dark thoughts and feelings your heart. Repent of them.
- Release to Jesus any wrongs made against you.
- Envision your whole being flooded with light.
- Thank God for renewing you. Shine His light to others!

BELIEVE
- Time for a Bible verse! Read one. Write it down.
- Contemplate it. Study it. Commit it to memory.
- Pray over this verse for insight and how to apply it.

BE JOYFUL
- Write down at least one thing you are thankful for and one prayer.
- Think of whom you can be a joy-giver to today and write down what you'll do for that person.

BEHOLD
- Resolve to face this day with eyes and heart wide open, with curiosity and a sense of wonder. God says, "Behold! I am doing a new thing!" (Isaiah 43:19, ESV).
- Enter into situations anticipating God at work. Write down your observations.
- Review the past beholding moments. Look for connections.

AFTERWORD

God is far more interested in developing our character than He is in enhancing our performance. Performance is a human creation and often a substitute for what should be a relationship with Jesus, something to fill in the gaping hole in our hearts that can only be filled with His presence. Striving is manmade. But we are not the suppliers nor sustainers of life, God is. And if we can learn how to rest in Him, to fellowship with the Spirit, to simply *Be* in His presence, then everything else that needs to be done will be done in its proper time. To quote Thomas Merton again,

> *"Sooner or later we must distinguish between what we are not and what we are. We must accept the fact that we are not what we would like to be. We must cast off our false, exterior self like the cheap and showy garment that it is. We must find our real self, in all its elemental poverty, but also in its great and very simple dignity: Created to be the child of God, and capable of loving with something of God's own sincerity and His unselfishness."[13]*

---

13   Merton, Thomas. Essay. *No Man Is an Island.* San Diego, CA: Harcourt Brace & Company, 1978, p. 203.

My prayer for you as you journey through this experience is that you would learn how to truly be the person God created you to be. I hope that in this process, you will discover the joy of living wholeheartedly surrendered to His plan for your life—not one based on human performance and lists of things to do, but based on Romans 12:1–2, which exhorts us to offer ourselves as "a living sacrifice to God, dedicated to His service and pleasing to Him." As we sacrifice our selfish desires and all of the things we feel we should be doing in response to our expectations and the expectations of others, we will continually open ourselves to God and His transforming work in our minds. He will ensure a complete, inward transformation—one that results in peace and freedom and joy—a *Plan Be* plan!

Throughout the seven Be-Attitudes, we've journeyed within and by the power of the Holy Spirit have learned to embrace life, to listen to our Lord, to let go of worries, and, through His peace, calm, and mercy, to be loved and to seek to love others. We've stepped into His marvelous light, that we might learn to live free, open, transparent, and unencumbered by the ways of the world. We've learned the importance of His seeking and soaking in His living Word, and to be people of prayer, gratitude, and joy. In this journey we're reminded of how the internal work prepares us for the external work—the outreach to others in kindness, generosity, favor, and love. Finally, in *Be*hold, as we live fully present, we learn to see life through spiritual lenses, opening up for us the amazing life He calls us to experience and share.

The banner over *Plan Be* and the purpose for which we live can be summed up in 2 Corinthians 5:14–15 (ESV):

"For the love of Christ controls us, because we have concluded this: that one has died for all, therefore all have died; and he died for all, that those who live might no longer live for themselves but for him who for their sake died and was raised."

In parting, my friend, I would like to pray this personal benediction over you. May you:

Give cheerfully
Love extravagantly
Share generously
Communicate openly
Live transparently
Care deeply
Welcome warmly
Reply kindly
Encourage specifically
Laugh heartily
Sow bountifully
Sing joyfully

"Finally, brethren, farewell.
Become complete.
Be of good comfort,
be of one mind, live in peace;
and the God of love and peace will be with you."
~ 2 Corinthians 13:11 (NKJV)

PLAN *BE* JOURNAL TEMPLATE

Throughout this book, I have mentioned the concept of jour-naling. To help you in your quiet time, I have created the template below, which can be used as a guide as you incorporate the Be-At-titudes daily. Or, it can be printed, copied, and used as a journal.

The first page includes each Be-Attitude for *Plan Be* ("BE") and the practices outlined in this book. The second page can be used as a planner and to-do list for each day ("DO").

In the spirit of "being before doing," the BE page should be used prior to starting your workday. Use the DO page for plan-ning, scheduling, and task management.

Under each Be-Attitude, there is space to journal thoughts, ideas, reflections, et cetera. (For *Be*lieve, it will be necessary to incorporate a daily Bible verse that you can meditate on (and memorize!).

BE

M   T   W   TH   F   SA   SU   DATE: / /

BREATH**E**   ☐ Big-3   ☐ Smooth-7   Prair:

BE STILL   Sacred word (to re-center yourself)

BELOVED   I know God loves me because…

BEAM   ☐ Repent   ☐ Release   ☐ Renew

BELIEVE   Daily Scripture verse to meditate on:

BE JOYFUL *always!*
PRAY *continually.* "Lord, I pray for…"
1.   Answered ☐ Date/Pg. Ref ___
2.   Answered ☐ Date/Pg. Ref ___
3.   Answered ☐ Date/Pg. Ref ___

Give **THANKS** *in all circumstances.* "Lord, thank You for…"
1.
2.
3.
…for this is God's will for you in Christ Jesus." (1 Thessalonians 5:16-18)

BEHOLD   What did God reveal to you today?
How did you see Him at work?

DO

pg. #

TIME	TRINITY	STATUS
(Schedule your tasks in the calendar by number)	Top 3 Tasks for Today)	
05:00	1.	☐
05:30	2.	☐
06:00	3.	☐
06:30		
07:00	**TASKS**	
07:30	4.	☐
08:00	5.	☐
08:30	6.	☐
09:00	7.	☐
09:30	8.	☐
10:00	9.	☐
10:30	10.	☐
11:00	11.	☐
11:30	12.	☐
12:00		

Pause: How's it going today? What prayers do you have?

12:30		
01:00	13.	☐
01:30	14.	☐
02:00	15.	☐
02:30	16.	☐
03:00	17.	☐
03:30	18.	☐
04:00	19.	☐

04:30   20.   ☐
05:00
05:30   Notes:
06:00
06:30
07:00
07:30
08:00
08:30
09:00

BENEDICTION: What has blessed you today?

Status: \ In Progress ✓ Completed ✗ Cancelled

ABOUT THE AUTHOR

Denny Hanrahan has been a believer in Christ for more than four decades and has navigated management in the business world for over 25 years through many trials and triumphs, diligently seeking answers from the Lord on how best to live and lead. Years of "thinking through his pen," resulting in stacks of journals, led to his desire to share  the peace and joy he learned in them with others.

Denny's passion for God's Word and his pursuit of greater intimacy with Him led to the creation of this work and Plan Be Life, LLC, whose mission is to cultivate a spirit of "Being before Doing" and "Success through Surrender." Denny has been married to his wife, Jill, since 1987, and has two adult children, John and Georgia. They currently reside in the great state of Texas.

www.plan-be-book.com

A free ebook edition is available with the purchase of this book.

To claim your free ebook edition:

1. Visit MorganJamesBOGO.com
2. Sign your name CLEARLY in the space
3. Complete the form and submit a photo of the entire copyright page
4. You or your friend can download the ebook to your preferred device

Print & Digital Together Forever.

Snap a photo

Free ebook

Read anywhere